BBC MUSIC GUIDES

HANDEL CONCERTOS

D0412805

BBC MUSIC GUIDES

General Editors: GERALD ABRAHAM & LIONEL SALTER

BBC MUSIC GUIDES

Handel Concertos

STANLEY SADIE

BRITISH BROADCASTING CORPORATION

Contents

I should like to acknowledge specially warmly the help of Anthony Hicks, who has generously given me the benefit of his detailed knowledge of Handel sources and has helped substantially towards the establishment of the true facts about Handel's self-borrowings and the dating of his works. He read over the draft manuscript and made many valuable suggestions. I am also grateful to Susan Wollenberg for information on a 'new' Handel borrowing and to Peter Williams for information on Handel's organ at Covent Garden.

S. S.

Published by the British Broadcasting Corporation
35 Marylebone High Street, London W1M 4AA
ISBN 0 563 10349 3
First published 1972
© Stanley Sadie 1972
Printed in England by The Whitefriars Press Ltd,
London and Tonbridge

Introduction

Handel was not primarily a composer of orchestral music. For the three central decades of his life (1710–39) he was first and foremost an opera composer; and for the last three (1730 to his death in 1759) he was an oratorio composer. All his organ concertos, and probably two-thirds of his concerti grossi, were written for use within performances of other works, oratorios in particular; and most would not have been written at all, we may be sure, but for the special needs of his oratorio audiences. He wrote few concertos in the years before the London operatic stage first claimed him; his preoccupation even then was the human voice. He never, in fact, cultivated the concerto as a musical form, in the sense that he cultivated the cantata, the opera and the oratorio. He may not even have been specially interested in it.

None of this makes his concertos less interesting or less important as a part of the repertory – Handel was a great composer, and it is not for nothing that his finest concertos and Bach's Brandenburgs are traditionally described as the twin peaks of the baroque concerto grosso. But it does help explain the nature of his concertos: their refusal to fall into consistent patterns; their improvisatory quality; their quite startling (to those used to the regular logic and clarity of Bach or Vivaldi) strokes of originality in design, in texture, in the nature of their actual material. It also helps explain his propensity to re-use chunks of old material, sometimes unaltered, sometimes radically reworked, and his not infrequent tendency to take considerable trouble over the surface and the bass of his music and leave it comparatively unpolished internally.

Handel's dependence on circumstances, his readiness to rely on his freedom of invention and his gift for the happy caprice, is reflected – in a manner as irritating to the scholar's tidy mind as it is stimulating to his receptivity – in his cavalier attitude towards his musical texts. He often revised his music, and his changes sometimes make it hard for us to talk in terms of a 'definitive' version of a work. We have to solve this problem as best we can in each case, and to learn to put up with Handel's large-scale carelessness, recognising that it is all an integral part of a genius which operated exclusively on a large scale, and which disdained to concern itself with minutiae.

The Early Concertos

It is not easy to talk of 'the early concertos' as such; partly because we do not know precisely when most of them were composed, and partly because those which we take to be early do not fall into a homogeneous group. For the purposes of this chapter, we take as 'the early concertos' the three with solo oboe and the so-called 'Sonata', which together form the final part of Volume 21 of the Händel-Gesellschaft edition,[1] and one miscellaneous work of uncertain provenance.

'I used to write like the devil in those days, but chiefly for the hautbois', said Handel of his youth to the flautist C. F. Weidemann. Not much oboe music has survived from his early years, unfortunately: there is a set of trio sonatas,[2] some of them very clumsily written, and attributable to Handel on only slender, highly suspect evidence. There are also three oboe concertos which are indubitably his own work, the first of which may be taken as fairly early. Their autograph manuscripts are unknown. The two in B flat were first published by John Walsh, London's largest publisher, in the fourth part (1740) of a miscellaneous concerto compilation called *Select Harmony*. The third concerto, in G minor, was not published until 1860, when it was stated to date from 1703. No evidence for that date survives; but it seems a reasonable guess, and might apply equally to the first of the B flat pair. The dating of the second, as we shall see, raises more complicated issues.

The first of the oboe concertos has always been the most popular: it is the most direct in manner, the most attractive melodically. The first of its four movements is an *adagio* of nineteen bars, quite simple and informal in its design. It is not specially subtle, though one might note the way that phrase-lengths shorten to provide a sense of accelerating activity. The *allegro* which follows starts with an eight-bar ritornello and what seems likely to be a distinctive solo theme; but the structure is free, almost improvisatory, with only the simplest recurrence of material and the texture mostly made up of three-part, triosonata-like writing for oboe, first violins and continuo, with a little harmonic padding. The *siciliana* has much charm and a touch of poetry; the type of movement is one which

---

[1] All references are to this edition; the form used will be *HG* xxi, 86–116.

[2] *HG* xxvii, 57–90; according to Burney (*Sketch of the Life of Handel*, p. 3), he made the above remark to Weidemann when shown this set.

Handel used extensively in his operas to portray pathetic situations, and though this brief piece has no such pretensions it does have a flowing melodic line, and its timing of cadence is exquisitely judged to deceive, then satisfy, the expectant ear. The texture is rarely more than three-part. Last, a minuet, marked *vivace* (not a particularly fast tempo in Handel's day): one of those happy, confident move-ments of a kind which no one but Handel ever wrote. The oboe and first violins are in unison; there are two strains, each repeated, the second ending with the same eight bars as the first, with a more emphatic final cadence.

With the second concerto the textual problems start. Its first movement exists in two forms: (*a*) in B flat, for strings (no inde-pendent viola part) and oboe; (*b*) in F, for strings (viola optional), oboes doubling the violins, and two solo horns. Version (*a*) also appears, in A, as the first movement of the Sonata to Chandos Anthem no. 7. In (*a*) the tempo is *vivace,* in the Chandos version *andante,* in (*b*) *largo. Vivace* and *andante* were close in contemporary usage, and the difference in (*b*) is accounted for partly by the treat-ment of the semiquaver passages – in one case soft, gentle inter-ludes, in the other fanfare-like passages for the louder, more cumbersome instruments. Even apart from the solo passages, limited by the natural horns' capacities in (*b*), the working in (*a*) is more refined in detail, and it may reasonably be taken as the later. The semiquavers alternate with French-overture-like dotted-rhythm sections; conceivably (*b*) is a discarded *Water Music* overture, or some such occasional piece, which Handel later decided could be rescued and put to use.

Another reason for taking (*b*) as the earlier is that the remaining movements of the oboe concerto are 'borrowed'. The fugue which comes second appears in a different form and key in a trio sonata, Op. 2 no. 5, for flute, violin and continuo,[1] and in virtually identical form as the second movement in Chandos Anthem no. 7; the two versions are similar up to half-way, but thereafter the concerto version is more closely worked, its texture better integrated (avoiding certain patterns more comfortable on solo instruments, as used in the sonata version). Again one may deduce that the concerto movement seems to be the later: had Handel been com-posing such a movement specifically for a concerto, he would

[1] *HG* xxvii, 125: this is Chrysander's numbering, which differs from that of the original Walsh publication (*HG* nos. 4–7 correspond to Walsh nos. 3–6).

doubtless have given the oboe something more to do than simply double the first or second violins. The remaining two movements, an *andante* and an *allegro*, are direct transcriptions from the overture to Chandos Anthem no. 5 (first version); they also appear in the trio sonata, Op. 5 no. 1. The *andante* – to which we shall return – started life in a 'Sonata a cinque' (in five instrumental parts), was rewritten in trio-sonata form, rewritten again for the anthem, and then transposed for this concerto (the supererogatory nature of most of the second violin part supports that order). The *allegro* is a cheerful 3/4 piece, with bustling semiquavers and lively dialogue writing; the soloist is reduced to duplicating one or other of the violin lines, with four bars' well-deserved breathing space in the middle. It seems clear that this concerto is a compilation, put together for publication; it could even have been assembled by one of Handel's copyists, or his publisher, from his instructions.

The third oboe concerto, in G minor, starts with a *grave*, dominated by arresting, jerky French-overture rhythms, and in a miniature ritornello form. The *allegro* which follows is easy-going music, similar to the equivalent movement of no. 1 in several ways – the lack of any real contrapuntal elaboration, the loosely defined solo-tutti relationship, the contrast between passage-work and thematic matter, the sudden changes of texture, the filling-in part for the viola (implying a possible trio-sonata origin). It is, however, superior in flow and design to the other movement. But there can be no doubting that it is an early piece. Third is a simple sarabande, the oboe accompanied in five-part harmony by the strings; its first strain is curiously extended from the expected eight-bar phrase to a nine-bar one. Were the lack of a reliable source to lead anyone into doubting the authenticity of this concerto – and there is no musical reason to do so – the content of the last movement leaves no room for doubt. It begins with a thematic idea which Handel used in a variety of forms and contexts – in an organ concerto, a trio sonata (Op. 2 no. 6, finale), and (reduced to a skeletal thematic outline) two other chamber works and a keyboard piece:

Ex. 1

Gerald Abraham[1] aptly calls such ideas 'generating themes'.

[1] *Handel: a symposium* (London, 1954), chapter 10.

Examination of its various forms throws a good deal of light on Handel's methods of work; considering here only the forms he uses in the concertos, and the closely related one in the sonata, it is fascinating to see how he modified the opening according to the medium: in the sonata, an expansive, modulating twelve-bar phrase, giving opportunity for an imitative reply from the second violin; in the organ concerto, a closed, compact phrase, also of twelve bars, as a terse statement of the material before an identical entry by the organ; in the oboe concerto, a simple ten-bar statement, leading to an informal oboe entry.

Two further works remain to be considered in this chapter. One may be dismissed briefly: the concerto edited by Max Seiffert and published as Concerto Grosso no. 30 in a practical edition linked with the Händel-Gesellschaft. Seiffert found the manuscript (not in Handel's hand) in an Electoral residence on the Düsseldorf–Hanover road, and concluded that Handel, who used that road, must have composed it for a music-loving Elector; but the internal evidence for authenticity is exceedingly slender and the concerto, for two horns, two solo violins, strings and double continuo, could be by any averagely competent German baroque composer.

The other work is the *Sonata a cinque*, sometimes called Violin Concerto in B flat, probably dating from Handel's Italian years. Handel returned to the material of the first movement several times: in the *andante* used in Oboe Concerto no. 2 and the Op. 5 no. 1 trio sonata, in Chandos Anthem no. 5 (two different versions), and in the oratorio *Belshazzar*; a related idea, in the minor mode, opens one of the Aylesford pieces for harpsichord. The versions in the *Sonata a cinque* and the Oboe Concerto are in B flat, the others in A. That the Sonata version is the earliest is borne out by the music itself – its rhythms are the simplest, and the opening theme is played first solo and then repeated tutti (such an opening, with a theme directly repeated at the same pitch, is natural to a concerto-like work). Further, the Sonata – for solo violin, first violins and oboe I, second violins and oboe II, viola and continuo – bears every sign of being an early piece. The finale apart, its form and style are not those of a normal baroque concerto. The first movement lacks the usual solo and tutti sections (there are only four bars of anything resembling solo passage-work), but the material is fascinatingly full of possibilities (as Handel evidently came to appreciate), and the dialogue between voices is closely worked. There is a short

9

adagio, nothing more than a series of chromatic chords (presumably a basis for improvisation), and a superficially lively, very Italianate final *allegro* – Handel's only attempt at a true violin concerto movement, and not one to provoke regret that he failed to exploit the medium further. As we shall see, he had better things to do in concerto form.

Opus 3

Handel's first published concertos were the set he and his publisher, John Walsh senior, called Opera Terza. They are not, of course, his 'third work', in any sense; he had behind him some twenty-five operas, half-a-dozen oratorios, many anthems, and countless other instrumental works. The custom of the time was to reserve opus numbers for published sets of instrumental works, which for the convenience of performers were normally issued in batches of six or twelve. In Handel's numbered works, even the solo harpsichord music was excluded, so that his Op. 1 was the dozen solo sonatas (melody instrument and continuo) first issued in 1733, his Op. 2 a set of six trio sonatas of the same year.

Op. 3 was published in 1734. Samuel Arnold, composer and editor of Handel's collected works in the late eighteenth century, thought they were 'chiefly composed at Cannons[1] in the year 1720'; Friedrich Chrysander, editor of the Händel-Gesellschaft edition, thought they dated back to Handel's period as Kapellmeister in Hanover, 1710–12. As we shall see, there is probably some truth in both theories; but the concertos almost certainly did not exist as such until shortly before their publication. A copy of the rare earliest printing[2] bears an 'NB': 'Several of these Concertos were perform'd on the Marriage of the Prince of Orange with the Princess Royal of Great Britain in the Royal Chappel of St James's'.[3] That marriage took place in March 1734, and Handel's serenata to celebrate the event, *Il Parnasso in Festa*, was given in the same

[1] The Duke of Chandos's mansion, at Edgware in Middlesex.

[2] In the Balfour Collection, National Library of Scotland, Edinburgh; see H. F. Redlich, 'A new "Oboe Concerto" by Handel', *The Musical Times* (1956), xcvii, 409.

[3] Supported by Sir John Hawkins; see *A General History of the Science and Practice of Music* (1776), p. 358.

month; possibly the concertos were assembled, largely from existing material, for performance at the wedding and in the intervals of the serenata performances. The astute Walsh might well have invited Handel to put them in the form of a set of six for publication, or indeed have done the job himself.

The disparate nature of the concertos in this set, however, need not be thought to lessen their collective musical worth. As so often in Handel's music, the 'borrowed' movements seem to fit uncannily well into their second (or third, or later) contexts. Only one concerto, the first, has no known borrowed material, but there is reason to suspect that this one, too, has some background history. One thing that eighteenth-century composers took seriously, indeed took for granted, was consistency over the key of a work: every piece begins and ends with the same tonal centre (not necessarily in the same mode; many works start minor and end major, or more rarely vice versa). Op. 3 no. 1 starts in B flat, moves quite orthodoxly to G minor for its slow movement, and quirkily remains there for the finale. Did Handel simply forget? Or is the concerto a hasty compound of previously existing movements? Or (conjecturally) did some kind of accident take place in Handel's copying office or Walsh's engraving workshop, with a B flat dance movement intended to round off no. 1 getting misplaced, so leaving no. 2 in B flat with two final dances and no. 1 with none?

However, the consistent (and rare) use of two viola parts throughout argues for the integrity of the concerto as it stands. It begins with an *allegro* (not so marked by Handel; it was too obvious to need to be said) of a thoroughly Italianate kind: unison strings announce the ritornello theme, built of arpeggios and scales and sequential figuration:

Ex. 2

Apparently it is quite conventional and square-cut, but in fact it is five bars long, rather than the usual (and rhythmically less interesting) four. The solo music in this movement is shared between a pair of oboes and a violin, a procedure more Vivaldian than Corellian; the Op. 3 set as a whole lean rather to the manner of Vivaldi and his German imitators than to Corelli – it was later, in his Op. 6, that Handel, following the English taste, used the more old-fashioned Corellian style. Still, in Op. 3 no. 1 he is far from orthodoxly Vivaldian. The sturdy, cheerful first movement is loosely constructed, quite unlike Vivaldi's more or less fixed formal scheme; there is no final appearance of the opening ritornello, let alone a central appearance in a related key, though the ritornello material is extensively used in the orchestral parts.

The outer movements call for two oboes, two bassoons, solo violin, strings and continuo; the slow movement also requires two recorders, and only one of the oboes has music to play. It is one of the most sensuous-sounding movements Handel ever composed. The rhythm has the gentle lilt of a sarabande. The recorders are usually supported by the bassoons, and there is a good deal of dialogue between wind and strings:

Ex. 3

Later in the movement this passage reappears, instrumentally re-arranged, with the recorders adding a soft halo to the strings, set against solo oboe and bassoon. There is also florid writing in dialogue between solo violin and oboe. After this, the finale seems a trifle perfunctory. It is a mere thirty-six bars long: a four-bar opening ritornello, a short episode for two oboes and bassoon, two bars of tutti, a slightly longer one for solo violin with varied accompaniments, three bars of tutti, a third and most ingenious episode for two solo bassoons (partly in dialogue with violins), then the four-bar closing ritornello. Not, perhaps, one of Handel's strongest or best proportioned concertos; but it has some good extrovert music in its outer movements, embracing a tender, warm-hearted slow one.

No. 2 is probably the best concerto of Op. 3. Its design is unusual but successful – a fast movement, a slow one, a fugue, and two dances; and it contains good examples of several characteristic Handelian veins. The opening *vivace* is a vigorous triple-time piece, the two solo violins chasing one another in dashing semiquavers (and eventually catching up with one another), while the remaining strings and the oboes give out a strong, decisive rhythm; later the texture elaborates, and there is a surprising moment just before the end when the violins break off and the oboes introduce a triplet rhythm. The virility and sense of direction of the bass line contribute to the movement's strength and structural clarity. The *largo* which follows has more of unorthodoxy, not least in the 'senza cembalo' direction in the bass part – it is figured as if for a continuo realisation, but it must be assumed either that the figuring was meant as an indication to the director (seated at the harpsichord) of the correct harmony, or that it was added as a matter of routine by the publisher (figures were often supplied by publishers' hacks, and can rarely be taken as authentic). 'Senza cembalo' does not, as is sometimes supposed, mean 'col organo'. The nature of the texture shows why Handel wanted to dispense with harpsichord sound: it is harmonically complete, it has a gentle, soft quality, and the cello figuration is likely to be better audible if the pitch gap between the bass and viola parts is left uninhabited:

After eight bars in this vein, the solo oboe enters at the top of the texture, with a plain melodic line; no doubt Handel expected it to be elaborated by the player.

The third movement is a fugue, but not a fugue that a Bachian would happily acknowledge as such. It is another typical piece of Handelian unorthodoxy:

Ex. 5   Allegro

As its first six bars show, there is not even the usual opening series of subject entries; moreover, the part-writing is often unconventional, and there are several points – points of climax, as usual with Handel – where the contrapuntal flow is stemmed in favour of more harmonic writing. Yet it is as closely worked as most Bach fugues. The thematic tags marked in Ex. 5 are amply developed (they appear in all but two bars of the movement) and there are several effective strettos (overlapping entries of the fugue subject). The movement was originally composed as part of the overture to the Passion which Handel wrote around 1716 to a text by B. H. Brockes; a somewhat different working of the same material appears as no. 3 of his *Six Fugues or Voluntarys for the Organ or Harpsicord*, published in 1735. The two dances with which the concerto ends, however, are new. Perhaps the first, a minuet (though Handel did not so title it), is a little less than brand new: its opening is prefigured in a number of earlier works, notably a recorder sonata – it is one of those characteristic 'generating themes'. Here it is continued with particular elegance and finesse, melodically, harmonically, and orchestrally. The final gavotte (again not so called by Handel) is a theme with two simple variations: in the first, the bass instruments have running quavers below the melody, and in the second the violins have a bustling triplet variant – a tuneful and rousing end to the concerto.

The Op. 3 concertos have traditionally been called the 'Hautboy Concertos' – a long tradition, dating back to their original publication; the title is a commentary on the rarity in England of concertos with important oboe parts. But it is slightly misleading, not only because none of them is an oboe concerto in the modern sense (like those discussed in the preceding chapter), but also because not all of them require an oboe in performance. No. 3 in G is for oboe or flute, solo violin, strings and continuo. It consists of only two movements, neither of them new. The material of the first dates back to one of Handel's earliest compositions in the English language, his Birthday Ode for Queen Anne, where it appears in a counter-tenor solo and a chorus; it comes again in a chorus in the Brockes Passion (for the crowd mocking Christ), and later still, in a more grandiose setting, in *Deborah* (1733). The instrumental version, in a characteristic blend of fugal and ritornello designs, was composed as the Sonata to Chandos Anthem no. 7, about 1718; with minimal changes, Handel used it in Op. 3 no. 3. It is a strong, attractive piece, well worth rescuing from the near-oblivion of its anthem context; harmonic tensions give it a powerful sense of forward motion, and the episodes – in which the soloists have running semiquavers against the steady quaver movement of unison violins – make their point without fuss and in shapely, civilised fashion. An eight-bar *adagio* (adapted from a chorus in the Chandos *Te Deum*) precedes the next movement; it consists of an oboe melody punctuated by string chords, and was so absurdly misprinted in the Walsh edition (a bar left out in the oboe part, and an extra one added later to make up the number) that it must usually have been played wrongly in the eighteenth century.[1] There are other slips – a bar omitted, another printed a third too high – in the fugue which forms the finale (see Ex. 8, p. 29). This movement started life as a keyboard fugue (no. 2 of the set mentioned above).

[1] See *HG* xxi, 31, which shows both the Walsh text and Arnold's attempt to rectify the mistake in his edition; Handel's intention can be restored by consulting the *Te Deum* for which the passage was originally composed, *HG* xxxvii, 76.

Although the subject (prefigured in a chorus in Chandos anthem no. 9) is arresting, its treatment is dull and repetitive, too dependent on sequence, and ultimately dry in effect. The orchestral version is further weakened by thinnish textures, for the violas merely double the bass line and the oboe is in unison with one or other of the violins. Handel could not have been very proud of this concerto.

Consideration of no. 4 demands a brief note on the bibliographical background of the set. Op. 3, as we have seen, was published in 1734. The main edition was advertised in December that year, but the preliminary one with the title-page 'NB' about performances at a royal wedding, must have appeared earlier in the year. The special interest of the earlier edition is that it contains a different concerto instead of the familiar no. 4 in F. The circumstances are odd. Handel, or Walsh, must have withdrawn the original no. 4 (which we shall call 4b) between printings. Is it really by Handel? did it get into the first Op. 3 issue by mistake? A mistake is not impossible: Walsh numbered all his publications, and Op. 3 and *Select Harmony* vol. 3 (in which this concerto also appears) are consecutive; so it is just possible that a careless printing operative confused two sets of punched plates, both of concertos in F, lying side by side in the workshop. Another possible explanation is that Handel included this concerto at first, because it had been played at the royal wedding, and then, when the no longer topical 'NB' was erased from the title-page plate, decided to substitute for it the much superior – and to some extent already popular – no. 4a, consigning the inferior piece to *Select Harmony* (along with concertos by Geminiani, Facco and another Anon.). That explanation is supported by the fact that Concerto no. 5 consisted of only two movements in the earlier issue, but had another three added for the later, again implying Handel's dissatisfaction with the set as it originally stood.

What of the evidence of the music itself? It is less conclusive than one might have hoped. There is no movement that Handel used elsewhere, and there are several technical solecisms – Handel was never specially careful about obeying the rules codified by nineteenth-century counterpoint teachers, but here he seems to have been more than usually negligent of them. There is first a *largo* in the jerky rhythm of a French overture, not of great strength but arguably Handelian in its two brief episodes with solo oboes and cello and in its final broadening. The *allegro* which follows is not fugal, but bustles along cheerfully in semiquavers, beginning very like Handel's sinfonia to *Acis and Galatea* (1718); there is solo music for two oboes, rather along the same lines as in Op. 3 no. 1, and some for violin too (not marked 'solo', but obviously so intended). Then comes a weak, uncharacteristic *largo*, for just the oboes, first violin, and a cello embroidering the continuo line; it is like a trio-sonata movement with added elaboration. The minuet-rhythm finale is an attractive piece which could conceivably be Handel's.

Op. 3 no. 4*a* is incomparably superior: it is all too easy to see why Handel wanted the concertos exchanged (if he did). The opening French overture, and probably the minuet-style *andante* which follows, date back to 1716: in June that year one of the performances of Handel's opera *Amadigi* at the King's Theatre was set aside as a benefit night for the orchestra; to show off the orchestra's talents, Handel supplied extra instrumental music, including this piece, on which account it was dubbed the 'Orchestra Concerto' or the 'Second Overture in *Amadigi*'. (Probably it was played between the acts, or to replace the Act 1 F major sinfonia.)

The *Water Music* was composed around 1716, and this concerto shows Handel in the same sturdily cheerful, extrovert vein. There is a short slow section in French-overture dotted rhythms to start with, then a fugue so gay, on a subject of such character and resilience of spirit, as to obliterate all academic notions of what a fugue ought or ought not be. It would be sheer pedantry to complain that the textures fall into harmonic patterning at the cost of contrapuntal integrity, or that the later subject entries are not carried through in orthodox fashion: the movement has a breadth of design and continuity of impulse which make such matters seem trivially irrelevant. As always, Handel bends pre-existing forms to his own purpose, approaching them with a characteristically English lack of dogmatism.

In this movement the oboes do no more than double the violins. In the minuet the first oboe has something of a solo part. This is a graceful little piece, which also exists in a keyboard version (in the Aylesford Pieces); the unusual layout of the bass part at the start implies that the keyboard version came first. The third movement, the only new one in the concerto, is again a sturdy *allegro*, semi-fugal, using another of Handel's favourite tags – one of its early uses is in 'The flocks shall leave the mountains', in *Acis and Galatea*, and here as there a sense of rhythmic propulsion is provided by the harmonic tensions inherent in the motif. This movement is mainly in three-part counterpoint, two equal upper parts set against a slower-moving bass, with the violas filling out the harmony; there is a brief episode for two solo violins.

There are resemblances between this D minor movement and the one in that key in the *Water Music* (see p. 67), and still more between the final *allegro*, another minuet, and various *Water Music* movements. The *allegro* too has an ancestry: its first part appears in the Op. 1 no. 5 flute sonata and the third collection of harpsichord pieces (published 1733), and both parts appear (separately) in the Aylesford Pieces. The extra elaboration of the orchestral versions suggests that they are the later, and one can well imagine that Handel, needing a concerto finale, would have arranged a piece from among his lesser keyboard works rather than start afresh. Naturally enough in an arranged keyboard movement, the second violin and viola merely provide a harmonic filling. But the layout of the middle section is unorthodox:

Ex. 6

The top line here is of course a gloss, not the melody, which is carried in the middle part by bassoon, second violins and viola. Handel uses this same texture in the *Water Music* (see p. 67).

No. 5, the only minor-key concerto in Op. 3, starts with a pair of movements taken from Chandos Anthem no. 2. The first is a severe, noble piece, setting triplets on unison violins against stern tutti chords – not quite as vast a tutti, however, as Elgar provided in his once-popular Overture in D minor arranged from it. As usual in music written for the orchestra at Cannons, there is no viola part, so Handel simply added one doubling the bass line an octave higher. The fugue which follows is again in three voices, the oboes doubling one of the violin lines; but it is one of the more orthodox and respectable of Handel's fugues. It has three main ideas – the downward scale of the opening, sustained notes across the rhythm, and a quaver figure – all of which are rigorously developed. This is a powerful movement, not in the least dry or academic for all its contrapuntal devices, but distinctly more serious in general feeling than the less 'learned' fugues like the one in the preceding concerto. A somewhat different working of the same material appears in the first collection (1720) of Handel's keyboard suites.

The remaining three movements, as we have seen (p. 16), were added between the first printing and the December one. Two of them may be new material, composed for the purpose – though the lack of independent viola parts (implying an origin at Cannons or in a non-orchestral form) should put us on guard against rash assumptions. The *adagio*, a mere fifteen bars, is nothing more than an interlude. The fugal movement following it comes from the Sonata of Chandos Anthem no. 6, a direct transcription, transposed down from E to D minor, and with the usual doubling viola added. It is again rather a severe piece, not unlike the other fugue in this concerto in its consistent contrapuntal treatment, though it is less broadly conceived. The finale is an *allegro* in gavotte rhythm, with a delicately witty touch – as for example after the initial unison playing of the theme, when the violins leave the basses half a bar behind, and then, as the basses make to catch up, move off upward instead of downward. There is a short middle section with a hint of the traditional musette drone-bass (see p. 47).

No. 6 has some good music, but not enough. Buyers of six concertos must have felt a little cheated at reaching the end so quickly. The two movements which make up this concerto in any case fit together indifferently. The first is a bold, dashing piece which Handel composed for use in the opera *Ottone*, probably for its 1726 revival rather than the première three years earlier. Bold in several senses: in the wide leaps of its line, in the unusually difficult passage-work for orchestral violinists, and in its chromaticisms:

There are solo episodes for oboes and bassoons. This movement is in D major, the finale in D minor. It is a version of a movement Handel used several times, and for this particular context he chose – for obscure reasons – a version in which the solo part was for keyboard (organ or harpsichord), which serves to emphasise the disparity between the movement and the rest of Op. 3. Probably the earliest working of this material – basing the argument on the music itself – is the one for solo keyboard in Suite no. 3 of the first collection; the earliest version in concerto style is the one with solo violin which appeared in the overture to the opera *Il pastor fido* (first version, 1712). In his two very similar later versions, here and in an organ concerto (see p. 60), Handel surprisingly restored only part of the virtuoso solo figuration from a violinistic form to a keyboard one. At each revision he shortened the movement and tightened up its structure; the result here is a lively, formally very clear-cut piece – but with little sense of belonging in even as spontaneously assembled a set as Op. 3.

The Early Organ Concertos

Unlike most great composers, Handel was an innovator. Not in the romantic sense, of an artist striving for new forms of expression to meet his inner needs, but in an almost accidental, or incidental, way – simply by remoulding existing forms to answer the requirements of new circumstances. His biggest creation was the English oratorio; another was the organ concerto.

Handel was, of course, trained as an organist from the time of his youth in Halle; his first professional appointment was as organist of the Domkirche there (not a specially demanding post, in a Calvinist establishment). There is a famous anecdote about his prowess on the organ as a young man in Italy, when in a contest his friend Domenico Scarlatti outshone him on the harpsichord but owned Handel his superior as an organist. According to Johann Mattheson, chronicler of early eighteenth-century musicians, Handel's achievement as organist was rivalled only by that erudite Leipzig figure J. S. Bach. Handel never held an appointment as organist in his London days, but his skill was famous. There are stories of him and Maurice Greene, in Handel's early years in London (when the two were still friends), spending hours in St Paul's Cathedral, where Greene would act as organ-blower simply for the privilege of hearing Handel at the console.

Handel's earliest work for organ and orchestra – possibly the earliest of all works for solo organ and orchestra – is the 'Sonata' he wrote in his Roman oratorio *Il trionfo del tempo e del disinganno*, a bright, lively single-movement piece with a certain amount of figuration of the kind he was later to use in his concertos. But it was another quarter of a century before the organ concerto proper came into being. It is a curious coincidence, though no more curious than the simultaneity of the discoveries of Newton and Leibniz, that in the very years when Handel was writing his first organ concertos in London, Bach, independently, was composing (or adapting) his first keyboard concertos in Leipzig.

Those twin pillars of English eighteenth-century musical history, Burney and Hawkins, both say[1] that Handel first played organ concertos in the intervals of performances of the oratorios *Deborah* and *Esther*. Those works were given in spring 1733 (*Esther* in 1732 as well). Burney also tells of Handel's playing the organ – though probably he was referring to solo improvisations rather

[1] 'Sketch of the Life of Handel', in *An Account of the Musical Performances in Westminster-Abbey and the Pantheon in Commemoration of Handel* (1785), p. 23, and *A General History of the Science and Practice of Music* (1776), v, 355.

than concertos – at Oxford performances of *Athalia* in summer 1733; among those present were two young composers, Thomas Augustine Arne and the violinist Michael Christian Festing, who assured Burney that 'neither themselves, nor any one else of their acquaintance, had ever before heard such extempore, or such premeditated playing, on that or any other instrument'. The first definite information we have on Handel's playing of organ concertos, however, is from an advertisement in the *London Daily Post* in March 1735 for a performance of *Esther* at the Theatre Royal in Covent Garden, promising 'several New Additional Songs; likewise two new Concerto's on the Organ'.

Why did Handel invent the organ concerto? It seems clear that part of its function, in the 1730s, was to supply an element of virtuosity, which was something conspicuously lacking in English oratorio performances as compared with those of Italian opera: the nature of the vocal expression was different, and so, usually, were the singers' capacities. Handel's playing was evidently an important attraction to the audiences, and the legend 'With a Concerto on the Organ' appears in many of his advertisements for oratorio performances from 1735 onwards. He continued playing organ concertos well into the years of his blindness. Burney wrote:

To see him . . . led to the organ . . . and then conducted towards the audience to make his accustomed obeisance, was a sight so truly afflicting and deplorable to persons of sensibility, as greatly diminished their pleasure, in hearing him perform.

During the Oratorio season, I have been told, that he practised almost incessantly; and, indeed, that must have been the case, or his memory uncommonly retentive; for, after his blindness, he played several of his *old* organ-concertos, which must have been previously impressed on his memory by practice. At last, however, he rather chose to trust to his inventive powers, than those of reminiscence: for, giving the band only the skeleton, or ritornels of each movement, he played all the solo parts extempore, while the other instruments left him, *ad libitum*; waiting for the signal of a shake, before they played such fragments of symphony [i.e. orchestral ritornello] as they found in their books.[1]

Improvisation had always made up a part of his performances, and it is safe to assume that it was one of the particular attractions to hear just what the bold and brilliant Mr Handel would play each time. According to Hawkins, he introduced each concerto with an improvisation:

[1] *Op. cit.*, pp. 29–30.

a voluntary movement on the diapasons, which stole on the ear in a slow and solemn progression; the harmony close wrought, and as full as could possibly be expressed; the passages concatenated with stupendous art, the whole at the same time being perfectly intelligible, and carrying the appearance of great simplicity. This kind of prelude was succeeded by the concerto itself.[1]

Before we look at the works themselves, a word on the kind of organ Handel composed for might be opportune. He did not have at his disposal, nor did he require, the large instruments with several manuals such as Bach used (if he had, the idea of the organ concerto might never have been conceived). English organs of this period were small, and nearly always without a pedal board. The one Handel used at Covent Garden Theatre had a single manual with Open Diapason (8′ pitch), Stopped Diapason (8′), Principal (4′), Twelfth (2 2/3′), Fifteenth (2′), Tierce (1 3/5′) and Trumpet (8′); when asked in 1749 by Charles Jennens (compiler of the *Messiah* libretto) to advise him on the plan for a new organ in his home, Handel suggested precisely the same plan (except that a Flute replaced the Trumpet, as reed stops needed frequent tuning, inconvenient in a country district) for what he called 'a good and grand Organ'. He did, however, present a rather larger instrument (two manuals with 21 stops, but no pedals) to the Foundling Hospital, for their chapel; there is no evidence that he ever played concertos upon it. It must be emphasised that the kind of organ Handel had in mind when composing these concertos was essentially on a chamber-music scale, soft though bright in tone.

In September 1738 John Walsh published the fifth book of a series called *The Lady's Entertainment*, described on its title-page as 'a Collection of the most Favourite Airs from the late Operas Set for the Harpsicord or Spinnet, To which is Prefix'd The Celebrated Organ Concerto, Compos'd by Mr Handel'. This, the first organ concerto ever to be published, was no. 2 of the Op. 4 set. About the same time an unauthorised, pirated edition of the six Op. 4 concertos appeared (or evidently it did; no copy is known). Walsh promptly advertised, on September 27, that

Whereas there is a spurious and incorrect Edition of six Concerto's of Mr Handel's for the Harpsicord and Organ, publish'd without the Knowledge, or Consent of the Author, This is to give Notice, (That the Publick may not be imposed on with a mangled Edition) That there are now printing, from Mr Handel's original Manuscripts, and corrected by himself, the same Six Concerto's, which will be publish'd in a few Days.

[1] *Op. cit.,* v, 413.

Three days later he paid 25 guineas to Handel, and within another week the authentic edition appeared, marked 'These Six Concertos were Publish'd by Mr Walsh from my own Copy Corrected by my Self, and to Him only I have given my Right therein. George Frideric Handel.' The orchestral parts to go with them followed two months later – most purchasers, probably, contented themselves with the solo part, which was laid out in such a way that the domestic musician could give himself a fair idea of the entire work even if he did not happen to have an orchestra to hand. The original issue bears no opus number; the concertos were first called 'Opera Quarta' in an advertisement early in 1739. The mention of the harpsichord on the title-page and in advertisements was, of course, partly a matter of sales promotion; but the concertos nearly all sound well on the harpsichord and must often have been heard on it, both domestically and in public. There is no reason why they should not be given as harpsichord concertos today.

The texts of some of the concertos as published by Walsh do not correspond exactly with those in various surviving manuscripts; in this chapter we shall take the Walsh texts, which Chrysander used in the *HG*, as the basic ones, and will note some of the more important deviations. And the concertos will be discussed in their order of publication (which was probably of Handel's own planning) rather than of composition; though it is possible, with some detective work, to establish with some degree of certainty just when, and for what context, each concerto was written.

Op. 4 no. 1 in G minor was probably composed for performance in *Alexander's Feast*; its use there is established by a note in Jennens's hand on a copy (now in the Flower Collection at Manchester) and by indications in the manuscript of the ode. It was placed after the air 'Thais led the way'. Whether it was played at the first performances early in 1736, or those a year later, is doubtful. The concerto's first movement, a *larghetto*, defies any attempt at conventional formal classification. The severe dotted rhythms at the start suggest something of the French overture; another ritornello theme, for unison strings, is entirely Italianate; the solo part itself – which contains only an outline, harmonically (with a figured bass part) as well as melodically – is woven into the orchestral material, borrowing ideas from it, subscribing ideas to it, and yet in a curious way remaining lofty and detached. It would be broadly true, but misleading, to describe the G major *allegro* which follows as more

24

regular. The movement starts with a sturdy 12-bar ritornello, strengthened by imitation between first violins, inner strings, and basses; it ends the same way, and in between there are snatches of the ritornello material. And the soloist uses the ritornello theme as his main point of departure for semiquaver passage-work. But most of the musical development is based on a new, slower-moving, minor-key idea introduced by the organ; the movement draws much of its force from the interplay of that idea and the cheerful bustle of the organ semiquavers, which progressively gain in brilliance. The *adagio* third movement, in E minor, is a mere ten bars, an organ solo (apart from the final phrygian cadence) marked 'ad libitum'; presumably Handel intended the given text to serve as a basis for embellishment. Finally, a 3/8, minuet-like *andante* with variations, in G major: the organ and continuo (bass string instruments and harpsichord) state each clause of the theme, repeated by upper strings; then all join together for two variations on the organ, the first a melodic elaboration, the second in more brilliant scales and arpeggios. Essentially it is a light, delicate piece: the only dynamic marks are *p* and *pp*. This movement also appears, without its second variation and in F, in an early manuscript version of the trio sonata published as Op. 5 no. 6.

The next two concertos are the two performed with *Esther* in March 1735. They evidently created a stir: a newspaper writer called them 'inimitable', and Handel's friend Mrs Pendarves wrote in a letter that they 'are the finest things I ever heard in my life'. Op. 4 no. 2 in B flat has always been one of the most popular, and rightly so. It starts with a few bars in arresting rhythms (drawn from Handel's motet *Silete venti*, probably written about 1729), designed, it would seem, to hush the audience. The material of the *allegro* comes from a trio sonata, Op. 2 no. 4 (first published in the early 1720s). The organ concerto version contains incomparably the finer and more subtle treatment. The supple, teasing rhythmic structure of the principal ritornello is specially remarkable – its opening 14-bar phrase is constructed $\frac{1}{2} + 2\frac{1}{2} + 1\frac{3}{4} + 2\frac{1}{4} + 2 + 2 + 3$. A similar flexibility and unpredictability runs through the entire movement. In outline, however, the form is more conventional than that of the corresponding movement of no. 1, with a regular key scheme: the first central tutti in the dominant, F, shorter ones in G minor and C minor, and a full-size final one back in the home key. Even then the movement is not quite over – the

soloist takes wing again, and has an option on a bout of improvisation before an abbreviated and emphatic tying-up of the movement
by the orchestra. The organ figuration, of a kind that lies easily
under the fingers but falls effectively on the ear, is substantially
altered and expanded from the sonata version, and the solo episodes
introduce a few fresh ideas, some in dialogue with the orchestra,
some to secure a better balance between the episodes. (It is perhaps
worth noting, for the sake of any light it may throw on Handel's
mental workshop, that the remaining three movements of the
Op. 2 no. 4 sonata are also related to *Esther*; they appear in the
oratorio's overture.)

The *adagio* which follows is a mere six bars: a flourish for the
organist's right hand, with harmonic punctuation from the strings.
This kind of dramatic, fanciful florid writing must surely represent
Handel's own improvisatory style; modern interpreters of the
concertos could profitably use this movement as a model for their
improvised adagios. A lively minuet – marked *allegro, non presto*, so
not excessively lively – ends the concerto; it is another delicate
little piece, much of it *p,* some of it *pp,* with a touch of wit in the
way unexpected things happen, like the sudden breaking-out of
the organ into rapid scalic passages, and most of all the *pp* ending.

Op. 4 no. 3 in G minor is something of a compilation, and
perhaps a hasty one; the fact that Handel returned to the concerto
and tinkered with it suggests as much. The main part of the first
movement, an accompanied duet for solo violin and cello with the
organ confined to a continuo role, appears in a trio sonata, Op. 2
no. 6; it is modified here to make it more concerto-like (there are
two brief cadenzas) and to allow for the fact that a cello was
replacing the second violin. The eloquent opening phrase can also
be found in an aria ('Ah! crudel') in Handel's first London opera,
Rinaldo, where it appears on oboe and bassoon. Handel's original
manuscript, and the Walsh publication, show the movement in this
string duet form; but in the manuscript Handel later made some
marks (in pencil, now only faintly visible) indicating that the organ
was to play the solo lines and, evidently, the bass line too – which
means that an organ with pedal board must have been available to
him (see p. 56).

The second movement of Op. 4 no. 3 is based on the 'generating
theme' referred to on pp. 8-9. This is its largest-scale working: a full-
size concerto-form movement, with the soloist taking the ritornello

theme as the starting point for his episodes. There are short central tuttis in D minor, B flat and C minor, before the closing one – interrupted by a solo episode, and later resumed – in G minor. A hint of the 'sonata form' of the future is provided by a secondary theme, given out in the relative major and later heard in the tonic (it does not appear in the other workings of the same opening theme). The third movement, in the original form of the concerto, is a twelve-bar *adagio* in 3/2 time, again with solo violin and cello parts; the material is rather like that of the recorder sonata Op. 1 no. 2, a resemblance not perhaps as insignificant as at first it may look, since the finales of the two works are close relatives. When revising the concerto, Handel removed this movement, asking instead for organ 'ad libitum' movements both before and after the preceding one.

The gavotte-rhythm finale is another movement of complex ancestry, and possibly further descent as well (see p. 59). Movements very like it appear in a whole host of works, including the opera *Agrippina* (composed for Venice in 1709) and two of the Op. 1 sonatas. When Handel first drafted it for the present work, he simply transcribed the Op. 1 version for orchestra, assigning the solo music to violin and cello; then (before publication) he reworked it for solo organ, elaborating it in such a way that the repeat of its first part became a variation. In this final form it is essentially a dance-like, light-textured movement, with the role of the orchestra confined to two- or four-bar phrases opening the movement and marking its cadences.

These two concertos, as we have seen, were given – perhaps the first time Handel played concertos in oratorio performances – in March 1735, probably on the 5th. Three weeks later Handel played a new concerto in a revival of *Deborah*, and only a further six days on (1 April) he revived *Athalia* 'With a new Concerto on the Organ; Also the first Concerto in the Oratorio of *Esther*, and the last in *Deborah*'. On 25 March he had completed the one in F, Op. 4 no. 4. That concerto has a peculiarity: its finale leads directly into a choral 'Alleluia' on the same material as its final fugue. That 'Alleluia' is the closing number of *Il trionfo del tempo e della verità*, a 1737 revision of the Roman oratorio which we met under a slightly different title on p. 21, and the concerto has consequently been thought to belong in that work. Alternatively, it has been placed in *Deborah*; but if that were the case both concerto and chorus must have been copied and rehearsed in a single day, which seems improbable. A likelier hypothesis is that Op. 4 no. 4 was composed, not for *Il trionfo* or *Deborah*, but for the revival of *Athalia*: and that turns out to be supported by Handel's own pencil annotations in the *Athalia* conducting score. It would seem, then, that Op. 4 no. 5 was the new concerto in *Deborah* given on 26 March and the 'last Concerto in *Deborah*' repeated with *Athalia*, while Op. 4 no. 4 was the new concerto in *Athalia* on 1 April (and that it became associated with *Il trionfo* only because of a later transplantation).

Op. 4 no. 4 is a popular piece, and one which typifies a specially happy side of Handel's musical personality – his extrovert sturdiness and good cheer, his resilience of spirit. The first movement's striding main theme also appears in a chorus in the opera *Alcina,* which Handel completed just a fortnight after the concerto; we have no means of knowing for which work the idea was conceived. It might be said that the movement's solo passage-work is conventional in layout, and that the invention is too dependent on sequence; yet the treatment is so fresh, the succession of ideas so agreeably fanciful, the phrase structure so varied, and the working so strong (the arpeggio of the opening is constantly woven into the texture, and there are a few bars of contrapuntal development just where most needed), that it emerges vital and well-knit.

The *andante* strikes a note of expressive delicacy unusual in Handel's instrumental music. The orchestra is marked *pianissimo*, without oboes or bassoons (not normally specified but always taken for granted as supplementing the bass strings), and also *senza cembalo* (bearing out that a continuo harpsichord was normally expected to be present). Against the *pp* strings the organ registration is specified: open and stopped diapasons and flute (though in fact the Covent Garden organ had no flute stop). The gentleness of the movement is sustained by the languishing suspensions in the orchestral harmony and the sweetly flowing semiquaver triplets on the organ; there is a little dialogue, but scarcely any interchange of material except for the unconventional stroke at the start where the organ announces the tutti theme as a solo before the strings assert their title to it. This movement ought not be taken too slowly, for it is followed by an *adagio* – a mere nine bars, organ solo until the last two: written as a melody with figured bass, it is marked 'ad libitum', which probably should be seen as an invitation to harmonic filling-in and only a little decoration of what is already a reasonably florid line. The finale is a vigorous fugal piece, on a subject very like that of the fugue in Op. 3 no. 3 (see Ex. 8); but this one is much freer and less orthodox, with the ritornello acting as the fugue's exposition and middle entries and the organ solos in effect its episodes, some with free passage-work and others using material from the fugue subject. The movement is of course complete without the choral 'Alleluia'; Handel adjusted the ending for the Walsh publication.

Ex. 8

As we saw, Op. 4 no. 5 was probably the new concerto given in *Deborah*. 'New' is perhaps not quite the right word. To compose the concerto, Handel had his copyist write out the recorder sonata in F, Op. 1 no. 11, and simply added supporting orchestral parts round it, sometimes filling out the recorder line with simple additional harmony. The first movement, a *larghetto*, is unchanged in outline; the orchestral parts happily add an occasional imitation, perhaps suggesting what Handel visualised a continuo player's doing. In the *allegro* second movement he added a five-bar orchestral ritornello at the start, the same music as the first five bars of solo; otherwise he used the orchestra merely to reinforce the final cadence of each half. For the brief *siciliana* he added a two-bar orchestral introduction and filled out the texture; for the gigue-style finale (altered from *allegro* to *presto*) he again added two bars at the beginning and a further two to round off each half. Few concertos can have been as painlessly composed. For all that, it is a pretty and delicate little piece, understandably benefiting from light, fluty registration. Formally its interest is, of course, practically non-existent; stylistically, it belongs some two decades earlier, with a marked Corellian flavour.

Sir John Hawkins wrote[1] that this concerto was originally composed as a lesson (i.e. solo movement) for the harp, and that no. 6

[1] *Op. cit.*, v, 356–7.

was a recorder sonata; his mistake has given rise to a good deal of confusion. It is in fact Op. 4 no. 6 that was originally for the harp, in which form it was used in February 1736 in *Alexander's Feast*, a setting of Dryden's Cecilian ode in praise of music – it stood for the musician of olden times playing on his lyre. Handel's autograph score is marked 'Concerto per la Harpa'; the music is in the same form as in the Walsh publication, where solo organ is specified. In fact its top note, e''' flat, is too high for most English organs – a contemporary version exists trimming the offending phrases, and Handel himself transposed the movement down a semitone for use in a different context. Handel's autograph score of *Alexander's Feast* indicates a concerto for harp; an MS organ continuo part (probably a copy of an autograph) is headed 'Concerto per il Liuto e l'Harpa'. According to a word-book published in 1736, probably for the original performances, the concerto was for 'the Harp, Lute, Lyricord, and other Instruments'. No version with more than a single solo instrument has survived, and the question arises whether one ever existed – it could be that the lute and lyrichord (a kind of sustaining harpsichord, patented in London in 1741, actuated by moving wheels instead of quills) were merely part of a specially planned continuo department.

The text itself does not exactly clarify these questions. The concerto is scored in pastel shades: violins muted, lower strings pizzicato, woodwind confined to a pair of recorders instead of the usual oboes and bassoon. The design of the outer movements suggests that some kind of revision has taken place, parallel to that in no. 5. Without its six-bar opening tutti, the first movement could stand as a harp sonata, for the orchestra is silent apart from fourteen bars of doubling the soloist – four at the end of the first strain, a couple to point a G minor cadence, and an eight-bar final tutti. Very much the same applies to the finale, where the orchestral music amounts to an opening eight bars of tutti, which could well have been added (it duplicates the harp solo), reinforcement of the three main cadences, and non-essential harmonic support in another passage. The central *larghetto* too is formally complete without the orchestra; even with it, it is strangely bare in texture. In fact some passages seem calculated for dialogue between a pair of instruments of which only one is present. Without any support from the source material, one might infer from the internal musical evidence that the work was originally conceived either as a harp solo, or as a sonata for harp and another instrument (perhaps lute or, just imaginably, Hawkins's recorder), or part each.

None of which makes it less delightful as an organ or harp concerto. As in no. 5, discreet registration is essential on the organ. Some of the actual textures, particularly the almost Alberti-bass left-hand figuration in the first movement, are unlike anything else in Handel. The invention itself too is unusual, rather four-square, but with charm and lightness. A small work, though of a kind that only a great composer could produce.

At this point, discussion of the organ concertos has to be interrupted to admit a lone concerto grosso, which belongs nowhere but fits at this point both chronologically and by virtue of its connection, like Op. 4 no. 6, with *Alexander's Feast*. The concerto in C, traditionally called the 'Concerto in *Alexander's Feast*', was composed in January 1736 and performed between the acts of the ode; it later found a place in Walsh's *Select Harmony* collection (vol. 4, 1740). A concerto grosso with solo parts for two violins and cello, it is an expansive work, starting with an eighteen-bar tutti, to which the soloists respond more lyrically. In the usual Italian style, the tutti and solo passages alternate in clear-cut fashion, with little interchange of material – the two types of material are developed separately rather than together, although the soloists intervene in the final tutti (as so often in Vivaldi), partly taking a share of the ritornello material but also with an eight-bar episode of their own.

The second movement is a brief, flowing *largo*, in which the orchestra does little more than add emphasis to the cadences; the thematic matter (dialogue on a dotted-rhythm figure) is carried in the solo parts. The third movement starts fugally, with a very four-square subject, but fugal textures are confined to the ritornellos, and in the episodes the soloists disport with increasing energy – the first is mainly in quavers, the second in quaver triplets, the third in semiquavers, the fourth and fifth also in semiquavers but with many more of them. An ingenious, quite enjoyable movement, but of no special distinction; and that could be said of the whole concerto up to this point. But the finale, a slowish gavotte (it is marked *andante, non presto*), possesses a poised charm quite uncommon in Handel: its melody, full of 'Scotch snaps', unwinds elegantly, to be followed by a graceful variation for the two violins.

This is a lightweight movement, but, underpinned by the solidity of a well-directed Handelian bass line, it raises one of Handel's less interesting concertos to a higher plane.

In 1740 John Walsh decided that he would like to follow up the success of Op. 4 by publishing a second set of organ concertos by Handel; the only difficulty was that Handel had not actually composed a second set – only two new concertos had been written up to the end of 1739, as far as we can tell. So Walsh, presumably with Handel's consent, had straightforward organ arrangements made of four of the Op. 6 string concertos, nos. 1, 4, 5 and 10 (see pp. 40–53). The second set was issued without orchestral parts; it was intended simply for the amateur who liked to play the music over on his own harpsichord or organ. Four of the concertos, then, represent mere arranger's hack work, and need no further consideration.

The first two, however, were – in part or in whole – conceived in the form of organ concertos. No. 1 in F is dated 2 April 1739; it almost certainly had its première two days later in the first performance of *Israel in Egypt*, 'With several Concerto's on the Organ, and particularly a new one'. No. 2 in A is undated: it could be one of the 'several new Concerto's on the Organ' given (or at any rate promised) in January 1739 at the second performance of *Saul*, unless that announcement referred only to the concerto-like solo organ part in the overture; more likely, it was the new concerto, 'on purpose for this Occasion', which Handel played in *Alexander's Feast* on 20 March 1739.

No. 1 in F begins with a *larghetto* (Handel originally wrote *largo*) arranged from the first movement of a trio sonata, Op. 5 no. 6. Op. 5 was published early in 1739; it would therefore be natural to assume that the sonata version came first, and, if natural assumptions are perilous in Handel, this one is borne out by a comparison of the scores. In the sonata we have a piece of writing in the classical two-equal-parts-and-bass manner, the voices mostly in dialogue, occasionally in parallel thirds or sixths. The concerto is relatively clumsy: the dialogue of two violins becomes one between orchestral violins and solo organ, with an extra phrase inserted to justify the tonal contrasts, and a bigger, more formal cadence, apt to the form but less apt to the content, is supplied at the end. There is no reason to imagine that the second movement, an *allegro*, was conceived in anything but its organ concerto form (it also appears in the Op. 6 no. 9 concerto – see p. 51). It is one of Handel's characteristically unorthodox movements, and demands to be described. The opening ritornello has a mere five bars, plus a two-bar echo, before the soloist interrupts; he is then himself interrupted (by the orchestra's imitating him) after two bars resuming for one more (again imitated), then steering the music into the dominant key, C major (imitated a third time). Then, in effect, the ritornello is resumed: the orchestra plays a new phrase, which is repeated in sequence by the soloist, then again by the orchestra which (with only semi-frivolous interventions from the organ) winds up the ritornello, but still in C, so that its end feels 'open' rather than 'closed'. This interweaving of solo and orchestra at the outset of a movement is something new in Handel, and serves to suggest a much closer and less formalised solo-tutti relationship; the first four concertos of Op. 4 had already shown various kinds of freedom, but not to the extent whereby the very backbone of concerto form, the opening orchestral ritornello, was broken.

In fact, it is no more than cracked: its rigid division of solo from tutti has gone, but not its equally important, indeed indispensable, function as statement of the movement's material. The main solo entry, as it happens, uses new material, rhythmically linked to the end of the ritornello – it is the figure which earned the concerto the first half of its nickname, 'The Cuckoo and the Nightingale'. This duly devolves into more or less conventional passage-work (Handel inserted an 'ad lib' marking after the cuckoo calls, which can only mean that he expected the passage-work to be treated quite freely; more 'ad lib' marks appear in the later solo episodes). The music turns to the subdominant for the first central ritornello, which predictably is interrupted; it moves on to G minor, at which point we have the 'nightingale' episode. There is a further tutti, again starting in the subdominant but sharply switching to the home key to provide a sense of recapitulation; then more close dialogue, another brief episode, and a decisive (uninterrupted) version of the five opening bars round the movement off. Not surprisingly, the detailed composition of this movement gave Handel some trouble, particularly the precise balancing of its sections. The version first published corresponds with the original state of his manuscript, but the manuscript also shows cuts, marked in his own hand; these were incorporated in the version published just after his death (with which printed orchestral parts were also issued), and there is every reason to regard the later version, altogether tidier and more succinct, as definitive.

After the second movement Handel asks, perhaps surprisingly because it involves transgressing the normal four-movement form, for an organ improvisation in the (also surprising) key of A. Probably nothing more is required than a flourish ending on an A major chord, the dominant chord of the D minor *larghetto* which follows. This movement, in the lilting rhythm of a *siciliana*, is again based on constant dialogue between the organ and the strings, with much variety of phrase-length and with soloist and orchestra each taking up phrases from the other and turning them in new directions. The finale is another reworking from the Op. 5 no. 6 trio sonata. That sonata's fourth movement is an extremely closely worked, semi-fugal *allegro*, every bar using material derived from the six-bar opening statement for first violin and bass. The organ concerto version follows the sonata one almost exactly for the first thirty-three bars (with an extra three inserted so that two ideas can be briefly extended in a way suiting the double medium); then comes a ten-bar solo organ episode, replacing six bars of further contrapuntal working, after which the versions converge for another eight bars – a central D minor entry – before the organ departs on more passage-work. It leads into a formal entry in A minor, made more formal than in the sonata version because a concerto movement needs clearer punctuation points than a sonata one. The remaining part of the movement follows the sonata version more or less exactly, with an eight-bar solo episode inserted before the final thirteen-bar tutti. Of course, the music is not transferred unaltered from one medium to another: it is extensively redisposed, both in textural detail and between orchestra and organ, and the bass part is simplified from what suits a single cello to what suits a less agile orchestral bass section. But the likeness of the two movements, and the plausibility of the adaptation, shows how closely linked are the instrumental forms of the period.

Handel re-used material from this concerto in the Op. 6 no. 9 concerto grosso, as we shall see in the next chapter. And he re-used the whole of the A major concerto, no. 2 of the second set, in the Op. 6 no. 11 concerto – not vice versa, as is generally supposed. The autograph of the organ version shows a number of changes, suggesting that Handel was still actually composing while writing it, whereas the autograph of the string version is more in the nature of a fair copy. Moreover, the string version is dated 30 October 1739 and (as we have seen) there is every reason to believe that the organ version was written earlier that year. Internal evidence supports the organ version's priority.

In either form this is undoubtedly one of the very finest of Handel's concertos, an expansive work full of original strokes. The first movement is marked *largo e staccato*; its dotted rhythms preserve something of the arresting quality of the opening of a French overture. This forms the basis of the 12-bar ritornello; the first solo entry consists of two sketchy bars, marked 'ad libitum'. Thereafter the structure is less formal. The opening music returns for two bars, but the organ then enters with a free, improvisatory line against it. Later it recurs in the dominant key (after an organ cadence, obviously designed for embellishment), and again becomes a background to an organ line; and the last two bars of the ritornello also reappear, as if conclusively. But in a quiet pendant the organ, lightly accompanied, carries further – to a brief 'ad libitum' – a repeated-note motif heard both on the strings (quavers and semiquavers) and on the organ (as fast as demisemiquavers; not easy to articulate unless at a slow tempo).

The *largo* ends on the dominant, and next comes the direction 'Organo ad libitum'. Considering that the movement to follow is an *andante*, it would be reasonable to imagine that what is needed here is not a simple flourish but a more fully developed fast movement. Handel was a famous improviser of fugues, and it may be significant that in the string version of this concerto he wrote at this point an *allegro* fugue, which he later used (in Op. 7 no. 1, p. 57) in an organ version.

The third movement is a triple-time *andante* in Handel's sturdiest vein: it sounds a trifle four-square, but in fact the bars of its main theme fall into a 3 + 2 + 4 pattern. Formally, however, it gives an impression of being less orthodox than it actually is, because of interruptions in the ritornellos and the variation applied to the main theme, so that episodes and ritornellos tend to elide. The episodic material in the first three-quarters of the movement is made up of running triplets. Then a ritornello in the subdominant switches abruptly to the tonic – closely parallel to the second movement of the F major concerto in this set; it is interrupted by the organ, now in semiquavers, and finally, after an 'ad libitum' (a brief cadenza is implied), the main ritornello theme appears at full length, with an extra four bars rounding it off.

Before the finale there is a six-bar *largo*, a sequence of cadences for the organ alone, marked 'ad libitum' and an obvious invitation to increasingly florid elaboration. The *allegro* which ends the concerto once again demonstrates the links between musical forms: it is an excellent example of the *da capo* aria in an instrumental incarnation. There is a four-bar ritornello, taken up by the organ and continued with witty dialogue passages, which eventually assume a form matching a phrase in the pendant to the first movement (bar 45). The ritornello in E, the dominant (surrounded by semiquaver passage-work), is based not on the opening theme but on a rhythmically very similar development of it, heard earlier; and the final one is by no means a literal repeat either – Handel's knack of providing an air of finality by making a couple of small changes in melody or harmony, or in tacking on a bar or two, is seen happily here. But that is not all: as in a *da capo* aria, there is a middle section in the relative minor key, ingeniously linked to the beginning of the movement to introduce the *da capo*.

It is dangerous to discuss Handel's forms too schematically, to impose upon them ideas of progressive growth or development. Yet the two Second Set concertos unmistakably show a more subtle, more unified relationship between soloist and orchestra than is seen in Op. 4. We shall see later (pp. 55 ff.) how Handel pursued these changes in his later organ concertos, those which remained unpublished in his lifetime.

The Grand Concertos

THE BACKGROUND

The late 1730s represent something of a watershed in Handel's life, and consequently in his music as well. Up to then his interests, and the entire shape of his career, had centred on Italian opera. He had been musical director of London's main opera organisation, the Royal Academy of Music; when that failed, he had worked in partnership with its former manager; when their partnership broke up, he promoted opera performances himself. His enterprises, and those of his rivals, had failed in 1737; Handel had some kind of mental and physical breakdown, but recovered fairly quickly. After that he composed only four more operas, and his interest in the English oratorio grew steadily. Eventually, in 1741, he put opera firmly behind him. He was an adept business man, and he now devoted his financial resources (which were considerable) as well as his musical energies to the promotion of the new form.

In 1739 he was still, in a sense, feeling his way. The first of his truly great dramatic oratorios, *Saul*, was composed and performed, along with several lesser examples of the species. But he was not yet wedded to the form, and perhaps had not yet realised how profoundly it was suited to his particular gifts. His choral works of these years are of various sorts: there are the Cecilian odes, *Alexander's Feast* (1736) and the *Ode for St Cecilia's Day* (1739); the pictorial, cantata-like *L'Allegro, il Penseroso ed il Moderato* (1740), and the biblical oratorio, largely choral, *Israel in Egypt* (1738). There was also a revival in 1739 of the serenata or pastoral opera *Acis and Galatea*. It was during that time, in a few weeks of white-hot inspiration, that Handel put on paper the twelve grand concertos (to use his own anglicisation of 'concerti grossi') forming his Op. 6,[1] partly because he needed instrumental items to add variety to his concerts, partly because he wanted to produce a set of works suitable for publication.

The normal publishing convention, as we have seen, was to issue works in sets of six or twelve. Handel's relationship with his publisher, the canny John Walsh, seems to have been particularly amicable about this time; the men must have recognised and admired each other's qualities. It could well be that Walsh, having told Handel of his high sales of concertos by Corelli, Geminiani and Vivaldi, and even by lesser men like M. C. Festing and Robert Woodcock, encouraged him to compose a set himself. Handel obtained a Royal Privilege for copyrighting his music in October 1739, naming Walsh as his agent (this was the only copyright protection a composer could secure, and it was necessary at a time when piracy was regularly practised and otherwise impossible to prevent or punish). He worked on the concertos during September and October. All the autograph manuscripts survive, virtually complete, and the dates they bear tell their own tale of intensive work and ebullient creative energy: no. 1, 29 September; no. 2, 4 October; no. 3, 6 October; no. 4, 8 October; no. 5, 10 October; no. 7, 12 October; no. 6, 15 October; no. 8, 18 October; no. 12,

[1] The opus number was not added until 1741, at the time of the second edition.

20 October; no. 10, 22 October; no. 11, 30 October. No. 9 is undated (26 October would seem a fair guess); that concerto and no. 11, as we have seen, are largely transcriptions of existing works. Perhaps the energy faded slightly at the end of this hectically busy five weeks. The day before no. 11 was finished the following advertisement appeared in the *London Daily Post*:

This Day are Publish'd, *Proposals* for Printing by Subscription, With His Majesty's Royal Licence and Protection. *Twelve Grand Concerto's*, in Seven Parts, for four Violins, a Tenor, a Violoncello, with a Thorough-Bass for the Harpsichord. Compos'd by Mr. *Handel*.
1. The Price to Subscribers is Two Guineas, One Guinea to be paid at the Time of Subscribing, and the other on the Delivery of the Books.
2. The whole will be engraven in a neat Character, printed on good Paper, and ready to deliver to Subscribers by April next.
3. The Subscribers Names will be printed before the Work.
   Subscriptions are taken by the Author, at his Home in Brook's-street, Hanover square; and John Walsh in Catherine-street in the Strand.

Publication by subscription was one of the standard methods at this time, and one which Handel often preferred (though besides Op. 6 he used it only for vocal works). Buyers evidently liked it too, for the sake of seeing their names printed on a list at the front in the finished publication – and it may have cost less than over-the-counter purchase. Musical historians also like it, for such picture as it gives of the music-buying public. The list in Op. 6 includes several members of the royal family, some composers and organists (like William Defesch, Henry Needler and Charles Weidemann), various of Handel's friends and patrons (James Harris of Salisbury, later a keen organiser of Handel performances, Bernard Granville, Charles Jennens, the Shaftesbury family), London theatre and pleasure-garden managers (John Rich of Covent Garden, Jonathan Tyers of Vauxhall), and many musical societies (five in London, others in Canterbury, Dublin, Lincoln, Oxford and Salisbury). It was not, by contemporary standards, an exceptionally long list, with 106 subscribers for 128 sets – the discrepancy because several subscribers, including the managers and some of the musical societies, took two, three or four sets, no doubt for performance by a larger orchestra than could read from single copies. We might infer from Tyers's four sets that the Vauxhall orchestra could include eight or more first violins and other strings in proportion when playing the concertos.

It would be still more interesting to know the scale on which

Handel himself performed them. We may be sure that he used two continuo instruments, normally two harpsichords or organ and harpsichord: Walsh's first edition had only one set of bass figures, but his second has a further set with the solo cello part. Handel used all the new concertos, or so we may safely conclude, during his concert season of winter 1739–40. His opening concert, on St Cecilia's Day (22 November), consisted of both the Cecilian odes, with an organ concerto and 'two new Concerto's for Instruments'; a Walsh advertisement on the day of the concert refers to the Twelve Grand Concertos in course of preparation and adds 'Two of the above Concerto's will be perform'd this Evening'. On 13 December the audiences could hear 'two new Concerto's for several Instruments, never perform'd before'. An advertisement on 14 February bears out that four of the concertos had been given; another two were heard at the end of the month, in the première of *L'Allegro*, one more at a revival of *Saul* in March, and a further one at *Israel in Egypt* at the beginning of April. The set was published on 21 April, and two more concertos 'never perform'd before' were given with *L'Allegro* two days later. As Handel is unlikely to have claimed premières for nos. 9 or 11, which his audiences would have recognised as merely new incarnations of old works, the other ten are all accounted for.

THE MUSIC

Handel aimed his Op. 6 concertos at a specific public, to meet a specific taste. That taste was an old-fashioned one. The favourite composer of concertos, as far as the England of 1739 was concerned, was Corelli, followed by Geminiani (1687–1762, a Corelli pupil, active in London and Dublin over many years). Corelli's concerti grossi – his Op. 6, too – had been published in Amsterdam in 1712, two years after his death; probably they had been widely known by then for a decade or more through circulation in manuscript. (They may have been composed as early as 1682, when the composer Georg Muffat heard Corelli playing concerti grossi in Rome; it is impossible to determine whether those were the same works or sonatas played orchestrally.) Handel's actual techniques are often close to Corelli's: the unpredictable, often quite loose structures, the trio-sonata character of the solo episodes, the tendency not to differentiate between the solo material and that of the tutti, the use of fugal movements and sarabande-like second slow movements. Characteristics like these place Handel's Op. 6 at the opposite pole from the Venetian concerto, of which Antonio Vivaldi (1678–1741) and Tommaso Albinoni (1671–1750) were the chief exponents. Vivaldi's concertos, almost without exception, are in three movements, fast–slow–fast, both the outer ones in a ritornello design of great clarity. That, by 1720, was recognised all over Europe as the up-to-date style of concerto composition; Bach, in Cöthen and Leipzig, modelled practically all his concertos on the Venetian pattern.

But Handel was more catholic, more wide-ranging; his personal style bore a stamp so strong as to be able to weld a great many diverse elements into an artistic unity, and his mind was so full of new ideas that to call his Op. 6 concertos 'conservative' – as they are in most aspects of analysable style – would be absurd. They draw on every existing musical type, large and small: the trio sonata, the aria, the French overture, the Italian sinfonia, the English air, the German fugue, the theme and variations, the dance (of diverse nationalities, even Polish).

And who but a composer of opera could have conceived the opening bars of the very first concerto (Ex. 9)? Essentially this is

Ex. 9

the music of a dramatic composer, the stern phrases of the orchestra set against the two solo violins, each phrase sloped downwards but the whole having an upwards gradient, with the music changing in character and to sustained texture once it reaches its apogee. This severe music is answered by an eloquent, sweet-sounding solo passage. The movement is short, and finishes most remarkably, chromatic, minor-key, drooping to its questioning final cadence:

The movement was originally drafted as a French-style overture to the opera *Imeneo*, much less individual and distinctive in invention than the final version. The *allegro* second movement, in Handel's typical bustling manner, follows directly. Only by Procrustean analytical methods can it be seen as a normal concerto-form movement; its final section, more like classical sonata form, contains a recapitulation in the tonic of material earlier heard in the dominant, and one could see the central ten bars as a rudimentary development. Its material consists mainly of the rather square two-bar phrase heard at the start and a half-bar figure used in series of sequences or dialogues. The ideas may not be specially interesting, but their treatment certainly is, with the ear constantly teased by the arousal of expectation and either its satisfaction or its confounding.

The third movement is a broad, dignified *adagio*, using scale figures and anapaest rhythms like the first movement. Burney wrote of it eloquently:

In the *adagio*, while the two trebles are singing in the style of vocal duets of the time, where these parts, though not in regular fugue, abound in *imitations* of the fugue kind; the base, with a boldness and character peculiar to HANDEL, supports with learning and ingenuity the subject of the two first bars, either direct or inverted, throughout the movement, in a clear, distinct, and marked manner.[1]

Fourth comes a fugue which, if it did not imply that Handel's fugues had more in common than they do, could be called typical. It is typical first in the colourful, arresting nature of its subject, second in its complete disregard of dogmatic fugal procedures, third in its lightly carried ingenuity. The fugal exposition consists of nothing more than a statement by the first solo violin, an answer from the second, and a tutti with the subject in the bass. Then comes an episode with dialogue of various sorts, harmonically rather than contrapuntally based – one of the dialogue figures, incidentally, is identical with a phrase from the second movement. The fugue subject returns, in the bass, and soon after appears shortened and inverted, to have a fresh exposition; later it comes both ways up at once. Just as the music seems to have gathered steam for a final statement, it breaks off abruptly in the middle of the subject and two *pianissimo* bars end the movement with a note of elliptical wit. A boisterous gigue, in the binary structure usual for a dance, ends the concerto.

No. 1 is a sturdy, virile concerto. No. 2 shows its gentler, more feminine character in its first bars – the *andante larghetto* first movement begins with a warm, flowing theme, richly harmonised. The movement falls into no recognised formal mould: its opening theme alternates freely with a solo motif which is sometimes smooth and gentle, sometimes firm and decisive. At the end there is a strange series of three cadences in sequence, with rests in between; some interpreters infer from the three-way symmetry that Handel expected the soloists to take turns at improvising brief cadenzas – a notion which, if indeed he held it, he might reasonably have made more explicit in the text he used for publication. The second movement is a semi-contrapuntal *allegro* in D minor, very much in trio-sonata style, with the two violins constantly imitating one another or running in parallel thirds. There is a certain spikiness to the invention, not entirely characteristic, but if the ideas themselves are short-breathed the movement as a whole runs with a firm sense of direction.

The third movement, like the first, sets incisive dotted rhythms against softer music, the latter here in a slightly faster tempo. Again harmonies based on suspensions in the inner voices greatly enrich

[1] *Account of . . . the Commemoration of Handel*, 'Fourth Performance', p. 102.

the effect. Finally there is a vigorous triple-time fugue on a fairly conventional subject (Ex. 11, lower line), for the most part quite orthodox – there are four voices, entering regularly, episodes which retain true four-part writing, and even some strettos of the kind beloved of fugal theorists. There are also a couple of episodes seemingly of an interlude-like character, but it later turns out that the new, slow-moving theme (Ex. 11, upper line) presented in them without contrapuntal garnishings is in fact a fresh counterpoint to the fugue subject.

Ex. 11

Handel at first intended this as a longer concerto: its autograph shows two additional movements, a minor-key fugue (placed second) and a gigue finale. Both later found places elsewhere in the Op. 6 set.

Handel's autograph of this concerto also shows parts for two oboes, as do those of nos. 1, 5 and 6. The oboe parts are written at the foot of the score, not in the usual position; in all likelihood they were later additions. Handel did not include them in the published texts, and there is no reason (least of all a musical one) to suppose that they are to be regarded as belonging to any definitive version of the concertos. Probably they were written for use when the concertos were performed in oratorios.

The third concerto, in E minor, contains some remarkable music. Its first movement, in sarabande rhythm, quickly establishes its seriousness, indeed gravity of mood; a gravity which may seem to be lightened by the tendency of several of its phrases to turn towards the relative major, if they were not usually turned back again, pessimistically, almost at once. The fugal second movement, a 12/8 *andante*, has an uncharacteristic subject, arresting (as usual), but rather by virtue of its melodic unorthodoxy than anything like rhythmic energy.

Ex. 12

The fugal treatment itself, however, is orthodox, as in fact the nature of the subject (perhaps paradoxically) predicates: the inner parts, in general, have a linear integrity worthy of Bach or any other composer to whom such things mattered.

The *allegro* third movement is more direct, more Italianate, than most of the music in Op. 6. Its sturdy four-bar unison opening might even be taken for Vivaldi. But although the solo sections are clearly marked off from the tuttis, both by differences in texture and decisive cadences, the actual material cuts across these divisions, and the tuttis, pervaded by the material of the opening four bars, are closely argued. The fourth movement (in G major) is described as a Polonaise, though it does not have many true polonaise characteristics. But a rustic folk-dance atmosphere is suggested by the drone bass, the rich, bagpipe-like scoring, and the rather repetitive melody of limited compass. The contrasting solo music is more aristocratic in tone, and the form is as close as Handel ever got to a classical sonata scheme, with a double-bar cadence in the dominant key and a formal recapitulation of all the material in the tonic. Finally there is a 6/8 movement, back in E minor, in fast tempo, but a rather serious little piece, with a lot of passing chromaticism and much dialogue between solo and tutti, often involving unexpected key changes.

Each movement mentioned so far, with the single exception of the chromatic fugue in no. 3, has some solo writing. No. 4 is largely an orchestral concerto. Its first movement, a *larghetto affettuoso* in Handel's broad, quietly grave manner, is texturally very simple, just a first violin melody above a bass in quavers (moving mainly by step, which strengthens the music's sense of direction) with the middle voices completing the harmony. The term 'affettuoso' carries a hint of the new *galant* style, which is reflected too in the nature of the melodic line with its leaning appoggiatura semiquavers. The *allegro* which follows is a fugue, on a characterful, slightly ungainly subject, longer than most of Handel's; it is interesting to note that to avoid tautology he contracts the exposition by abbreviating the viola entry (and incidentally having the bass one in the tonic rather than the dominant). Most of the fugal argument is stringent and orthodox, and even the passages of solo-tutti dialogue, though short-breathed, are strictly derived from the subject. The movement's sombreness is driven home by the ending, with the violins and violas dark-sounding on their lowest strings.

The F major *largo* is Handel at his serenest, sublimest and (which may be taken for granted) simplest. The bass instruments move in steady crotchets (the music is in 3/2 time, in the idealised sarabande style traditional in the third movement of four); above it the first and second violins duet gently, imitating one another, the lines intertwining, one stealing softly into prominence as the other pauses. The violas merely enrich the harmony. Finally comes a lively *allegro*, a reworking of an aria ('È si vaga') from the draft of the opera *Imeneo*, which was lying half-written in Handel's study in the autumn of 1739. The aria (marked *andante*) is quite loosely constructed, and a fairly light piece, for a secondary soprano; the concerto movement on the other hand is extremely tight in structure, its ideas thoroughly worked out, and its two thematic germs (one of six notes, one of five, in similar rhythms) placed in a wide variety of contexts and subjected to a wide variety of treatments. The interjections and the snatches of dialogue have a touch of wit; but the predominant sense of the movement is serious, with its persistent minor tonality, its melodic phrases often inflected by an unexpected flattening, above all its coda – the music reaches a cadence, and a lonely solo violin states the main theme, joined by the second and then by soft sustained chords which hint at distant keys before returning to a melancholy *pp* throb in A minor.

Just before embarking on Op. 6, Handel had finished composing his *Ode for St Cecilia's Day*, whose three-movement overture (a French-overture style *larghetto* and fugue, followed by a short minuet) provided a useful quarry for Op. 6 no. 5. Like much of the *Ode*, the overture's main thematic ideas are drawn from the keyboard *Componimenti musicali* by Gottlieb Muffat, published earlier the same year. Five movements of the concerto were composed by 10 October; subsequently – perhaps after hearing the concerto at a concert – Handel decided to add a final minuet. (The sheet on which he added it happens to contain the minuet and the rejected trio from the *Ode* overture, and the reworking of the trio as the finale of Op. 6 no. 3; but probably that has no significance in the concerto's textual history.)

In the brilliant-sounding key of D major, no. 5 is a lively, extrovert piece. The first movement is adapted from the *Ode's* French-style overture by the addition of a dramatic pair of prefatory bars for solo violin, and by a characteristic tightening-up of the material later on (again to stronger dramatic effect): it moves in sharp dotted rhythms and in rapid little scalic phrases, full of arresting gestures, with a virile swagger rather than pomposity. The fugue – broadly identical with that in the *Ode*, with three bars added – is on a four-square subject, in nature more harmonic than contrapuntal, and with an easy rhythmic swing. The movement is not so much loosely constructed as sectional; each idea comes to a clearly defined end, and a new one starts. It is a cheerful movement, without a hint of earnestness.

The third movement is a *presto*, a *moto perpetuo*-like binary piece in 3/8 time, the scurrying semiquaver patterns broken only at cadences. It is as near to a scherzo as anything Handel wrote. Then comes a typical 3/2 *largo*, dignified and Corellian, with the soloists initiating each idea and the orchestra adding its weight to round it off. The fifth movement is another light, brilliant and wholly characteristic piece, for all that its first theme hints at the sort of nagging figuration of a Scarlatti harpsichord sonata (indeed it resembles a particular sonata from the collection published in London in 1738) and its secondary one at Telemann's most amiable kind of passage-work. What makes it unmistakably Handelian is the balancing and integration of these ideas, and above all the harmonic purposefulness – the way the bass line moves, with a clear sense of where it is going and when it is due there, and the discords between the upper voices which by their need to resolve propel the music onward. These descriptions could, perhaps, be applied to a dozen or so Handel movements; but their use here is of so virtuoso a kind that it delights in its own right, like any other kind of virtuosity. Finally the minuet, which in essence is a variant of the *St Cecilia Ode* one, but with a much more direct and striking melodic line; more suitable, in fact, for variation treatment, which is what Handel gave it – first a restatement of the melody, ungarnished, but with a running bass, and second with the melody put into a running quaver pattern. For all the brilliance of the preceding movement, the warmth and sturdiness of the minuet finale make (as Handel must have recognised) a much stronger conclusion.

With the next concerto, no. 6 in G minor, Handel again had second thoughts about the ending. It was at first to be in four movements, the last a gavotte; eventually it had five, the gavotte being rejected in favour of two new movements. The more substantial ending is necessary partly to restore the balance of the

tonality after the long third movement in E flat. The first movement is one of the darkest Handel composed. It is a 3/2 *largo
affettuoso,* with brief solo passages, concerned not with grace of line
but with the expressive power of harmony and of string texture.
Once again, whenever a key-change to the brighter relative major
promises, the music turns back, and usually downwards in line, to
G minor melancholy; and it closes with all the string instruments
at the lowest, most sombre part of their compass. Then follows a
severe chromatic fugue, angular and closely worked, with no
suggestion of Handel's usual cheerful unorthodoxy.

'Musette' is the title of the third movement, a poised and deeply
poetic 3/4 *larghetto.* It is unrelated to the gavotte-like musettes of
Bach's keyboard suites and Handel's *Alcina* overture, but like them
hints, if distantly, at a dance with a drone accompaniment (the
musette was a form of bagpipe popular in the seventeenth century).
The sombre tone of the first movement is echoed at the
musette's opening:

Ex. 13

This dark sound is at once set against the higher tones of the soloists.
The movement is a long one, 163 bars in all, but it falls into four
clear sections, on an *ABCB* pattern, with *B* a continuation and
extension of the music of *A,* and *C* a contrasting section in C minor,
with steady semiquaver passage-work above rhythms from Ex. 13.
According to Burney,[1] Handel sometimes used this movement, a
special favourite, as an interlude in oratorio performances.

[1] *Account of . . . the Commemoration of Handel,* 'Second Performance', p. 54.

After this a substantial fast movement is needed, as Handel evidently recognised: though Burney says that in performance he often omitted both the fourth and fifth movements. The *allegro* fourth movement (with only a single solo violin) is a striding, Italianate piece, but a good deal subtler in form than its models – for example, in the way that the opening tutti seems to be repeating itself but leads off instead into passage-work, first orchestral, then solo. The movement has a central tutti in the dominant key; thereafter the solo episodes and tuttis become more closely interwoven, and there is no formal closing tutti though plenty of orchestral music in G minor to set the key balance to rights. Last is a brief, somewhat bluff 3/8 *allegro* in binary form, rather too fast and too angular in line to be called a minuet. It has resemblances to the finale of the Op. 4 no. 2 organ concerto, with its bustling triplets.

No. 7, the only purely orchestral concerto, starts with a short, grave *largo*, a mere ten bars; then comes a lively fugue on a subject that no composer but Handel, surely, would have dared use (Ex. 14*a*). The four-note figures in the last bar, together with variants derived by raising the first note an octave and a further extension (Ex. 14*b*), provide enough arguing matter to sustain a fairly light-textured movement of a hundred bars.

Ex. 14(a)

The next movement is a 3/4 *largo*, with a chromatic theme and a sustained four-part texture; the inner parts, supplying little more than harmonic sustenance to the texture, are typical of music conceived in terms of an expressive melody and bass.

The *andante* which is placed fourth is not (despite the views of many German conductors) a slow movement. It moves at a steady amble, without a strong sense of where it is going, and showing an inclination to pause frequently at cadences; but it goes along pleasantly, with some delicacy of line and attractively managed modulations. This too looks like music conceived in melody-and-bass terms. That does not necessarily mean that it comes from, or was intended for, a different work: the scrapped gavotte of no. 6 survives solely as a melody with bass – though possibly it offers more opportunities for interesting inner elaboration than Handel found space for in either the *largo* or the *andante* of no. 7. Much the same could be said of the Hornpipe, a cheerful binary movement with some boldly shaped lines and teasing rhythms, which ends this concerto.

If an earlier origin may be suspected in parts of no. 7, with the first movement of no. 8 suspicion is replaced by certainty. This concerto, in C minor, is the nearest Handel came to composing a 'concerto da camera', that is, a concerto made up of dance-style movements. It starts with an *allemande*, on the normal binary pattern; the polarity between first violin and bass at once hints at the music's keyboard origins – and in fact the basic material comes from Suite no. 2 in Handel's third collection. The brief, dark-toned, quite dramatic *grave* is manifestly a true concerto movement, its material based on solo-tutti contrasts. The *andante allegro* third movement is almost certainly original, even though the spritely four-note figure which dominates it goes back to a quartet in Handel's Venice opera, *Agrippina* (1709):

Ex. 15

Andante allegro

It is a curious piece, much dependent on a range of textural devices, particularly the exchanging between soloists and orchestra of its two main ideas (themes would be too exalted a word – the four-note figure, and a throbbing quaver pattern). To attempt to relate a movement like this to traditional concerto form would be impossible: all they have in common is a key scheme, which is anyway basic to most movements of the period.

The brief fourth movement, an *adagio* of twenty bars, starts (Ex. 16, overleaf) with a phrase (i) which anyone familiar with Handel's most popular opera, *Giulio Cesare*, would at once have recognised (ii); when the reminiscence ends, the music declines in interest. The *siciliana* fifth movement recalls his operas too, in general rather than in particular, for this kind of music appears regularly in pathetic situations; in fact, Handel first used this material in a movement composed for the oratorio *Saul* but rejected it at an early stage. Hints of phrases to appear in two *Messiah*

Ex. 16 (i)

(ii)

movements, the Pastoral Symphony and 'He shall feed his flock', can also be picked up. There is a particularly inspired stroke at the end, where against the final tutti the solo violins play rich counterpoints, which gradually assume the centre of the stage so that the ritornello material is suspended, to be resumed, *piano*, after the violins have carried their ideas to a conclusion. It is an uncommonly eloquent ending. There is a short binary *allegro*, with a touch of polonaise rhythm about it, to end with; a neat, crisp piece, its textures made unusually lucid by the doubling of the second violins and violas on a single (and rather wilful) middle part.

The ninth concerto is the only one lacking a date in Handel's autograph, probably because its last movement (where he usually wrote the date) was transferred from another concerto. It contains less fresh composition than any other; only the first of the six movements was actually designed for it. That movement is experimental, like many of Handel's; but unlike most it is manifestly unsuccessful. Nothing happens in its twenty-eight *largo* bars, except that a succession of harmonies is played. Apologists have suggested that Handel intended some kind of elaborate improvisation as a foreground to this background; but no composer in his senses publishes a piece demanding the insertion of the principal ideas at the performers' whim – baroque performing freedom did not stretch that far. We have already met the second and third movements in their original versions, in the organ concerto in F from the 1740 set (see pp. 32-4). The *allegro* is not only deftly and inventively transferred from one medium to another; it is also substantially expanded and its material further concentrated. In the first place, the organ's role in the dialogues is not simply handed over to the string soloists; sometimes it is, but sometimes the organ solos become the tuttis, the orchestral phrases the string solos. Sometimes, too, extra echo phrases are added. The 'cuckoo' effects which give the organ concerto half its nickname are eliminated in favour of simple repeated notes, first solo then tutti, exploiting the difference of colour and weight. The 'nightingale' effects are replaced too, by material from the ritornello and the adapted cuckoo; interestingly, Handel follows the same key scheme, having a tutti in G minor where previously the nightingale music had started in that key. And, at the point where the solo and tutti ideas had previously been intermingled, the same principle is followed in a more extensive treatment. Brilliant semiquaver episodes replace the final organ solo (partly 'ad lib'), and the movement is more tightly drawn together by an extra section on the repeated-note figure just before the closing tutti. In its original version this was a formally adventurous, imaginative movement; its later version retains those qualities but with a design both broader and better disciplined. Similar changes, but on a smaller scale, are applied to the *larghetto*; the first forty bars contain the same music, but differently distributed between solo and tutti, and the end of the movement is strengthened by at least a hint of a re-capitulation of the opening (there had been none before).

For the fourth and fifth movements of the concerto Handel turned to the overture of the half-written *Imeneo,* and transposed it from G to F. The fourth is a straightforward *allegro* fugue, without solo episodes, on a lively, helter-skelter subject, worked in (for Handel) strict fashion. The fifth is a minuet, transcribed with a few small changes; it had originally been in the major mode, but he adjusted it to begin in the minor and switch, oddly but not ineffectively, to the major just for the final eight bars. Last comes a binary gigue, newly written for Op. 6, but originally for the other concerto in F, no. 2; Handel evidently decided that no. 2 would be better without it, and simply transferred the movement to no. 9, where the minuet alone might have made a perfunctory ending.

No. 10 in D minor starts with a French overture, much in the manner of Handel's opera overtures: a severe movement with sharp, ejaculatory rhythms, and a fugue – the subject, of a kind Handel seems specially to have liked, starts with a pithy phrase, then runs off into semiquavers (the one in no. 9 is similar). It is a type which conveniently allows dramatic, arresting entries in the course of the fugue yet leaves the composer a good deal of freedom. This one is a strong piece, closely argued, ending with a brief *lentement* back in spiky French-overture rhythms. The next movement, marked *Air, lentement*, is in sarabande-like rhythm and of uncommon nobility and austerity, with some near-modal touches hinting at an antique style. Its phrase structure is formal and statuesque, but that is the nature of the piece, which is severe rather than warm or eloquent despite the softer nature of the solo passages.

There is something of the French-overture-and-suite about this concerto, and that provides the clue to its unusual movement scheme. The pair of *allegro* movements standing third and fourth have more than a hint of an *allemanda* and *corrente*; indeed the first of them would fit tolerably well both under the hands of a harpsichordist and into the format of a baroque keyboard suite. The second is more extended, more inventive, more like a true concerto movement. It is also extremely ingenious. There is no normal ritornello theme; the opening is shown in Ex. 17. The bass figure (*x*) is used as a contrapuntal point, and the octave leaps of the second bar are worked in as another idea for contrapuntal treatment of an easy-going kind.

There are still a couple more musical ideas to come; the movement is liberal in its material, but knits together pretty well by virtue of its rhythmic momentum, a strong feeling that all the material belongs to the same family, and the sheer sense of fun and

surprise that runs through it. For the finale Handel turned to major tonality – though this movement was at different times in D minor and B major (as finale to no. 12). In its final version, reached, no doubt, during the 1739–40 winter season, it is a cheerful and straightforward dance-like *allegro moderato*; each half is played twice over, followed by a variation with repeated violin semi-quavers.

No. 11, probably the last of the set to be completed, is largely an arrangement of the A major organ concerto, no. 2 of the second set; the organ version was published later but composed earlier (see pp. 34-5). The string version is much more carefully worked out in detail, with an independent viola part, much of the rhythmic notation more precise (the differences offer some clues, if ambiguous ones, on performing practice), and with several changes in layout and passage-work to accommodate the different character of the solo instruments. The organ 'ad lib' passages within the movements are also altered, assigned to the first violin and mostly now accompanied. In the three movements coming from the organ concerto, the first – now *andante larghetto* instead of *largo* – is otherwise unchanged except for the insertion of half a bar to point the last 'ad lib' and cadence more effectively; the long *andante* gains four bars (an effective anticipation by the soloists of the penultimate tutti); and the lengthy *allegro* in *da capo* form is exactly as before. Between the first movement and the *andante* comes a short *allegro* fugue, fairly loose in structure, breaking off two-thirds of the way through for a new fugal exposition on an elaborated version of the first two bars of its subject (this movement was referred to on p. 35; we shall meet it again on p. 57). A six-bar *largo* precedes the *andante*; the same movement (marked 'Organo ad libitum', and obviously meant as a basis for improvisation) comes in the organ version, but there following the *andante*. Whereas the organist is expected to understand the meaning of its normal dotted rhythms, in the version for orchestral players the sharp rhythms are made explicit by a different notation.

The twelfth and last concerto begins with another of those movements which uses the idea of the French overture – jerky, arresting rhythms to catch the listener's attention – without actually being one. It is a short *largo*, laid out to set the soft sound of the soloists against the tutti. The first *allegro* is a virile piece in Handel's best *moto perpetuo* manner, with a steady bustle of semi-quavers – at first on the solo cello, then on the violins, orchestral and solo. Any attempt to analyse a movement like this on a basis of standard concerto form shows only how little Handel subscribed to the conventions of his day. For a start, the principal idea is at first a solo one; it recurs first (in the dominant key) also as a solo, but later recurrences (in the relative major and twice in the tonic) are orchestral, which adds greatly to the effect of cumulation and rhetorical force. The intermediate material is little more than passage-work, but the rhythmic momentum and sense of harmonic direction, as well as the adeptness of the string writing and effectiveness of the scoring, make this one of the most inspiriting movements in the set.

And the *larghetto* which follows contains the most beautiful melody in the set. It is a broad, simple, regular 3/4 melody in E major, in two strains, with a wide span, not unlike the famous minuet in the overture to the opera *Berenice* (1737) in its quiet gravity. After its statement each strain is twice varied, like the minuet ending no. 5, first with a running quaver bass and then with the melody itself in quavers. After that, dashing off into a fast movement would surely have broken the spell too abruptly; Handel provides a short, grave *largo* to lead into the fugue which ends the concerto. The fugue subject derives from Zachow, who had been Handel's principal teacher when he was a boy in Halle; perhaps Handel was remembering a piece he had played almost half a century earlier, or even one of his early contrapuntal exercises. Certainly it is not among his cohesive or freely-flowing, or his more resourceful, fugues. But its gigue rhythms provide a spirited ending to the concerto and the set.

The Late Organ Concertos

Handel's late organ concertos – as the ones to be discussed in this chapter may conveniently, if not with absolute confidence, be called – consist of the set posthumously published as his Op. 7 and the miscellaneous works included in vol. xlviii of the Händel-Gesellschaft edition. They raise problems quite different from those raised by the works already discussed. The orchestral concertos of Op. 3 and Op. 6 and the organ concertos of Op. 4 were published in Handel's lifetime, with, almost certainly, his own imprimatur. The texts issued by Walsh may be disputable in detail, but they are genuine. Handel, at some stage, was prepared for those works to go out into the world in the form they did.

Op. 7 is another matter. It is a collection put together after his death, published (by the younger Walsh) in 1761. We do not know for certain who prepared the set for publication, but it is not unreasonable to suppose that it was J. C. Smith, Handel's long-standing friend, secretary and in effect chief of his team of copyists. If anyone was in a position to supply texts to Walsh, it was Smith; if anyone was in a position to know what Handel's muddled manuscripts really meant, it was Smith again. But although Walsh's Op. 7 texts may not be as bad as has sometimes been suggested – certainly there is no reason to imagine that returning now to the surviving autographs would produce anything better or more 'authentic' – the fact remains that the concertos were never put into a definitive form. In a sense, nor were the Op. 4 concertos, where details were left to be improvised; but the Op. 7 concertos have gaps too, and they are not, like those in Op. 4, always entire movements. Moreover, at several points the Walsh version conflicts with surviving autographs; sometimes it is the sole authority for a text, even for the arrangement of movements. Obviously there is room for doubt about Handel's precise intentions, and still more room for doubt whether his intentions were in fact precise. *Faute de mieux*, it must be best to take Walsh's texts on trust (as far as they go, and barring actual mistakes); they may well be based on the versions Handel actually played during the oratorio performances of his late years, as remembered by Smith.

Op. 7 no. 1 in B flat at once raises a further puzzle. According to organ historians, the only English instrument with a pedal board at this date was the one in St Paul's Cathedral. Handel did not play organ concertos in St Paul's; he played them in a theatre. Op. 7 no. 1, in which a pedal part is specified, and which is unplayable as it stands on an organ with no pedal board, was finished in February 1740 and must surely have been the 'new concerto on the Organ' given at the end of that month at the Lincoln's-Inn Fields Theatre in the première of *L'Allegro, il Penseroso ed il Moderato*. This was Handel's only season at that theatre, where some kind of pedal organ must have been available; in which case it seems likely that the alternative text of Op. 4 no. 3, where his pencilled directions imply the need of a pedal (see p. 26), was prepared for the same season.

We shall see that the Op. 7 concertos are even less regular in design and treatment than those of Op. 4; also that they are mostly rather larger in scale, in both a physical and an expressive sense. No. 1 is the largest of them all. The first two movements form a massive double ground-bass structure, built on the basses shown (*a* in the first movement, *b* in the second):

Ex. 18 (a)
Andante

(b)
Andante

The ground's first four notes are the basis of an introduction, in arresting dialogue; dialogue treatment continues above the full ground, but organ and orchestra are soon integrated – the strings supply the ground, the organ makes a crescendo of elaboration above it. When the music moves to the dominant key, the ground is used only sporadically, but it retains its grip on the structure in that its unifying presence is constantly felt. The movement twice echoes a much earlier Handel ground bass, from his Suite no. 7 for harpsichord – the opening of the suite's Passacaille appears in the concerto (its bass slightly modified), and the 'ad lib' which precedes the final tutti borrows a later phrase. This leads to the reappearance of the fanfarish dialogues from the movement's start, with an unmistakable sense of coda-cum-climax.

The climax is resolved – an extraordinarily bold stroke – by the second movement, an *andante* like the first, but much stricter in its use of the ground. In 3/4 time, it is of course in the familiar metre of the traditional chaconne or passacaglia, and there is a clear feeling of moving from an unconventional, rhetorical movement to one developed in a more normal and orderly way. It is extremely orderly. To start with, the organ gives out five statements of the eight-bar theme, each precisely echoed by the orchestra. They become progressively livelier: first, even quavers; then anapaest figures; then triplets; fourth an angular line in syncopated rhythm; and finally perky anapaests again. At this point the idea of orchestra echoing organ is dropped – the next expected echo is a distorted one, and then the organ has four solo variations (two touching on minor keys, two in brilliant semiquaver figuration). The orchestra rounds off the movement with a final emphatic variation, and with an *adagio* cadence in F to lead to the next movement.

At this point a D minor organ improvisation is indicated in the autograph, but the edition moves straight on to a D minor *largo*, a rather sombre movement in 3/2 time with hints of ground-bass procedure in the stark string octaves and arpeggio-based lines. After that there is another discrepancy between autograph and printed edition. Handel gave a shorthand indication that he wanted a fugue to be played, a version (transposed up a semitone, and shared between organ and orchestra) of the fugal movement in the Op. 6 no. 11 concerto – the only movement of that concerto which does not derive from no. 2 of the second set of organ concertos (p. 35). It has to be admitted that the organ-and-orchestra medium sits unnaturally on the piece. A lusty *bourrée*, with virile dotted rhythms, ends this noble concerto.

No. 2 of Op. 7 was completed on 5 February 1743, and must surely have been the new concerto given at the première of *Samson* later that month. It starts with a French overture, a slow movement in jerky rhythms, though with a typically English-style compromise in its gentler ten-bar solo episode; the fugue which follows is uncommonly ingenious, preserving the vestiges of ritornello form in a well-developed movement, with a fully argued fugal exposition and formal central and final tuttis acting as a framework for episodes, which include a couple of organ 'ad lib' passages and a good deal of brilliant solo writing (one rather empty section was cut – by Handel or his editors ? – between autograph and edition). It all seems very characteristic; yet in fact the fugue subject and most of the ancillary contrapuntal material have lately been shown to be by Gottlieb Muffat, not from his *Componimenti musicali* (one of Handel's favourite sources) but from a piece now known only in an obscure Viennese manuscript which Handel could never have seen. After an organ 'ad lib', the finale again draws on Muffat (this time in the *Componimenti musicali*) for its opening ideas. It is an unusual piece, alternating a sturdy tutti with solo music, partly pastoral with bagpipe-like sonorities, partly in running triplets.

The third concerto of this set was probably Handel's last instrumental work, composed during the first four days of 1751; on 1 March he played a 'New Concerto', presumably this one, to follow a performance of *Alexander's Feast* and to precede the première of *The Choice of Hercules*. It is sometimes called the 'Hallelujah' concerto because of the similarity of its opening phrase to the *Messiah* 'Hallelujah' chorus (though no other link is known between this concerto and *Messiah*). In fact, it originally lacked its 'Hallelujah'; Handel's draft score shows that the 'Hallelujah' material was an afterthought and that the movement had been planned to begin at its present third bar. This movement is one of the most intricately worked, most carefully balanced of any that Handel wrote. It has several thematic ideas, of which the 'Hallelujah' phrase is the least important – also the least representative, for the general manner is more intimate than rhetorical. There is much detailed writing in semiquavers and semiquaver triplets for the soloist, each solo having a strong sense of direction, leading at what is unmistakably the right moment to a brief tutti. The tonal structure is unusual, with only a brief spell of the dominant key, a substantial return to the home key (B flat) at the centre of the movement, then a long spell around G minor before the final return home.

After the first movement, Handel wrote 'Adagio e Fuga ad libitum'. Possibly he meant 'Adagio ad libitum, e Fuga', for he may not have wanted an improvised fugue immediately before the *spiritoso* movement, which itself begins fugally. This again is a finely worked movement with plenty of ideas, and it has some oddly sudden changes of mood – for example when the lively subject at the start (borrowed from Habermann) turns into a sombre phrase on the violins' bottom string, or at the mysterious moment when the music comes to a halt above a pedal for the violins to fan outwards in repeated quavers. Bold strokes like these are the hallmarks of genius, of the composer whose underlying serious cast of mind cannot always be suppressed. The concerto ends with a straightforward minuet, or possibly two. The *HG* text gives two, but the second, bound into the autograph at a later stage, may not have been intended as part of the concerto.

The history of Op. 7 no. 4, once again, is uncertain. Its movements were almost certainly composed at different times; the 1761 publication is the sole authority for linking them. Possibly the first movement dates back to 1733. It survives in two forms, one with both solo organ and continuo organ (it has sometimes been called 'Concerto for two organs' and treated as a separate work).[1] Handel used two organs in his 1733 *Deborah* performances; if this movement originated then, it may be the first he performed in London, and the begetter of the series. It is a D minor *adagio*, as dark-coloured, as gloomy a piece as any Handel wrote. There are divided cellos, each doubled by a melancholy bassoon; the music is low pitched, and these two baritonal voices imitate one another. In time it rises, and finally there is a dramatic, rhetorical organ cadenza. The second movement is a straight crib from the trumpet concerto in Telemann's *Musique de table*, set 2 (published in 1733; Handel's name is on the list of subscribers to the edition). Or nearly straight: Handel adds bars here, subtracts them there, and often shores up the bass-line. Telemann's garrulity disappears; the music acquires a strength, a moment, that he never achieved unaided. To see a cheerful but trite phrase transformed into a strong, succinct one, it is necessary only to compare the two versions of the opening bars (Ex. 19, overleaf).

Looked at in detail, the structure of the Handel movement is undeniably scrappy: there is no attempt at any kind of interesting relationship between solo and orchestra, and the 'ad lib' markings at the ends of solo passages can only lead to further loosening of the form. Yet there is a good swing to the music, and Telemann's

[1] *HG* xlviii, 51; the two-organ version has an alternative ending, completing the music in the home key (the other version is designed to lead direct to a second movement) and so making it self-sufficient.

Ex. 19 (a) Telemann Tempo giusto

(middle parts omitted)

(b) Handel Allegro

bright trumpet writing goes well on the organ. Next there is an organ 'ad lib' movement (presumably a slow one is required; Handel did not specify), and finally another version, identical in plan and substance, slightly simpler in detail, of the 3/8 D minor movement which we met in Op. 3 no. 6 (p. 20). It is perfectly possible that all the movements of this concerto had been composed by the mid-1730s but, had they been put together to form a whole, the concerto might have been included in Op. 4 (in preference to no. 5 or no. 6). More likely Handel grouped them – if at all – only in his later years: perhaps for the Occasional Oratorio performance on 14 February 1746, advertised 'With a New Concerto on the Organ' – though Op. 7 no. 6 could have been the work heard then.

Op. 7 no. 5 was finished at the end of January 1750, and was no doubt the new concerto given in the première of *Theodora* at Covent Garden on 16 March. Aptly for the sombre oratorio, it is in G minor. At first it may seem a scrappy piece, with its short (mainly two-bar) phrases and its choppy dialogue between organ and strings. But there is a good deal of virility to the invention, and ingenuity in the way an idea from the ritornello is treated as the solo theme – Handel finds opportunity for unexpected juxtapositions of key and interchanges of material, and the effect is often quietly dramatic.

This movement is followed by three bars marked 'Organo ad libitum', with the bass provided – whether the given passage is intended as the bass of the whole, or merely of the ending, it is impossible to say. It leads to B flat major, for an *andante larghetto* on a two-bar ground, played thirty times in all, including repeats; the strings play nothing other than the ground while the organ overlays it with new melodic matter or rapid passage-work. Handel marked it 'piano continuando', with a *forte* only at the last appearance of the ground. Another three-bar organ 'ad lib' leads back to G minor for a minuet, for orchestra with no solo part; and finally (in the publication but not in the autograph) there is a gavotte, another version, rather more fully developed and with no solo organ part, of the one in Op. 4 no. 3.

Nothing is known of the composition or first performance of Op. 7 no. 6: it could have been given with the Occasional Oratorio, though possibly the handwriting and paper of the autograph imply a date about two years later, contemporary with *Solomon* and *Susanna*. One might regard the first movement as somewhat perfunctorily composed: there is no thematic link between the ritornello theme and the organ passage-work that fills most of the intervals between its appearances. There is an 'ad lib' second movement, and a strange finale – a binary-form structure (with interesting counterpoints when the theme descends to the bass in the second half), then the whole played again with the insertion of three organ solos, with only the first bar and the closing cadence of each actually composed. The invention, with quirky rhythms and characteristically strong harmonic propulsion, is quite intriguing, but the effect of the whole is disastrous unless the soloist's sense of style is uncommonly keen.

Three further organ concertos remain: the so-called two-organ concerto referred to earlier, and the two printed after it in *HG* xlviii. The first of these, in D minor, is entirely based on the recorder sonata in Telemann's *Musique de table*, set 1. In its opening movement, marked *andante* (Telemann's only direction was *cantabile*; Handel seems to want a moderate-speed movement, and not apparently a *cantabile* style), severe, mainly unison ritornellos alternate with free episodes in a style and figuration derived from Telemann's recorder writing; only occasionally in the later solos is the style distinctively organ-like. One is left feeling that Handel did not take sufficient trouble to make something new and interesting from his model, though the 'ad lib' markings at the end of most of the solos (more than the *HG* score shows) suggest that the autograph, as usual, may not be a precise representation of what he really wanted. Next (again not in the *HG*) comes a request for a pair of 'ad lib' movements, an *adagio* followed by a fugal *allegro*. Finally, a jig-like *allegro* based on Telemann's finale: here too some of the figuration is copied from Telemann, but more, in a truer organ style, is added, and although the binary structure is retained the key scheme is altered. This is not one of Handel's better concertos. Although it sounds more like Handel than Telemann, its material is too closely derived to allow of the flights of imagination that mark out Handel's best music.

Finally, the long and strange concerto in F. The source problems of this work are immensely complex, and there are good reasons for believing that it was never intended as a unique, mammoth organ concerto in seven movements (the second an 'ad lib'), which is the form of its first edition (printed by Samuel Arnold in 1797 as part of his collected edition of Handel's works, and followed by the *HG*). The only sources are Arnold's edition and a solo organ part, in Handel's autograph, containing the first pair of movements (a French-style 'Ouverture' followed by an *allegro*), an 'ad lib' indication, the fifth (*andante*) and the seventh (a version of the march – by friend Muffat – in *Judas Maccabaeus*). In the first and seventh movements the organ merely doubles the orchestra, with no solo music of its own; in the fifth, it does have solos and also some silent bars – for which Handel, in a different manuscript, provided filling-in passages so that the piece could be played as an organ solo. It seems, then, that we may really have two distinct works here, which Arnold mistakenly linked because they have a common source: movements 1, 2, 5 and 7, as a solo organ work or a concerto; and movements 3, 4 and 6. These last have come down to us only in Arnold's version, which is clearly a botched-up one, based on the third double concerto (see p. 65). He seems to have presumed that the organ part should replace one of the two wind choirs, whereas the result is far more logical if it replaces both. Without authentic source material, that hypothesis cannot be proved; but the idea that Handel derived two normal-size organ concertos, rather than one mammoth one, from the third double concerto does not seem implausible. Discussion of the music itself must await the next chapter's survey of the double concertos in their original form – though 'original', as we shall see, is perhaps not quite the right word.

The Double Concertos and the Outdoor Music

Handel's last three purely orchestral works are the concertos known as the 'Concerti a due cori'. In fact they are for three 'choirs' of instruments: two wind groups (two oboes and bassoon, with two horns as well in nos. 2 and 3) and the basic string orchestra and continuo. Their colourful and festive character has led writers to conjecture that they were designed for some sort of ceremonial or outdoor occasion. More probably they were intended, like most of Handel's concertos, for use at oratorio performances; and the evidence, both internal and external, tends to bear this out.

First, the external. Looking down the list of 'new concertos' advertised in Handel performances, there are just three not yet accounted for: one in each of the oratorios composed in the wake of the '45 rebellion, *Judas Maccabaeus* (1 April 1747), *Joshua* and *Alexander Balus* (9 and 23 March 1748). The internal evidence, as we shall see, strongly suggests that the double concertos were composed after the middle of the 1740s. Further, a contemporary copy of no. 3 is marked 'Concerto in the Oratorio of Judas Maccabaeus'. The others must surely belong with *Alexander Balus* and *Joshua*, though we cannot tell which was given with which: that no. 1 includes material from the former may argue equally in either direction.

The music of nos. 1 and 2 is all adapted from earlier material. One may well ask whether Handel expected his audiences to recognise what they heard; were these concerto-interludes designed as excerpts from familiar works, or was this merely a matter of his refurbishing old ideas to save himself time and labour? No answer is possible. Some movements, like well-known *Messiah* choruses, must have been recognised at once; others, like reworkings of opera arias of a quarter of a century before, would surely have been unfamiliar. The whole business represents another baffling aspect of Handel's psychology.

No. 1, then, starts with a transposed version of the slow section of the French overture to *Alexander Balus*: possibly a surprising start to a work heard within that oratorio, and hardly less surprising if first heard two weeks before the oratorio's première. Instead of the customary fugue, the next movement is a transcription (with a brief cut) of 'And the glory of the Lord' from *Messiah*; the wind instruments play the chorus parts, the strings a slightly adjusted version of the original string parts. The result is inspiriting enough, but scarcely sounds like a true concerto movement. The same applies to the next movement, the exultant chorus from *Belshazzar* which represents the Euphrates rushing along its new path. The short fourth movement, a *largo*, is a thorough reworking of an idea which Handel used in his opera *Ottone*. Next is another chorus, a two-section movement full of bustling semiquavers at first, then moving into a formal fugue; it comes from *Semele*, with a brief cut in the middle. Again neither style nor form seems like Handel's orchestral music. Finally there is a Menuet, its material drawn from an aria in *Lotario* with some hints too of a song in *Alexander Balus*.

No one can pretend that this concerto stands as any sort of artistic whole; yet the stuff of it is good, and it makes diverting listening. In no. 2 Handel added a pair of horns to each wind group: and, right from the opening bars, he used the two groups anti-phonally (which he rarely did in no. 1). The first two movements hark back thirty years to the first version of *Esther*: the French overture-like 'Jehovah is crowned', with a solo horn replacing the alto Israelite, comes first, with a fresh and shorter ending to make a clearer-cut break; the following chorus, full of fanfare-like figures and vigorous string scales, is transcribed virtually un-changed (omitting the original middle section and repeat). Then comes an adaptation of 'Lift up your heads', from *Messiah*, with the original antiphony of the first half of the chorus (high voices versus low) adapted to the two wind choirs, at first with some minor adaptation of the material too. But in the main it is a literal tran-scription; the short dialogue-type phraseology of the original, in the second half as well as the first, is well suited to splitting between antiphonal choirs, and the ring of four horns, often high in their range, enriches the sound splendidly. Handel now turned back to *Esther*, transcribing a mournful chorus in *siciliano* rhythm to form a *largo*. The fifth movement goes back still further, to the Birthday Ode for Queen Anne of 1713, for its underlying ground-bass theme (it appears too in the 1732 version of *Esther*); the movement, however, is so much extended, and so fully reworked in instru-mental terms, with special attention given to the provision of idiomatic and effective horn parts, that it is virtually a new piece. Most of these arrangements of choruses hint at their origins in their style of orchestration, usually with one or both of the wind groups 'singing' the choral parts; this one discloses its sources less obviously. And the effect is grandiose and stirring. The concerto ends with a movement which gives the two leading oboists a good deal of brilliant passage-work; the tutti sections are based on a chorus from the Occasional Oratorio.

The third concerto, in F major like the second, seems mostly to have been freshly composed. Its Ouverture has material in common with Handel's 'Fitzwilliam Overture' for two clarinets and horn, but the next three movements are – as far as we know – original. The relationship between the two wind groups suggests, more clearly than anywhere in nos. 1 or 2, that the music was conceived in antiphonal terms, and in these particular colours. For example, the first *allegro*'s main tutti material is made up, first, of horn-like arpeggio figures and, second, of a rhythmic-contrapuntal phrase in which the two wind groups take turns at doubling the strings; its most important solo idea appears on the strings with bassoons doubling the violins an octave below. The succeeding movement starts with sixty-two bars of direct dialogue, in one-bar, two-bar and occasionally four-bar phrases, between the wind groups; the strings join in for a 24-bar tutti to round it off. The effect with the wind choirs placed well apart is very striking. Next is a brief D minor *adagio*, leading into another antiphonally conceived movement – but the contrasts are not always between the wind groups, and sometimes they cut across the more obvious orchestral demarcation lines. It is in an exceptionally extrovert vein, with the exuberance of some of the *Water Music* and perhaps, in its jubilant repeated notes, a reflection of the exultation in *Judas Maccabaeus*. The finale, a brilliant gigue starting with fanfare-like music for the horns, is based on material from the opera *Partenope*. This third concerto is undoubtedly the most unified and the most carefully composed of the three, and certainly the only one in which there is a satisfactory relationship between the forces used and the music itself.

There remain for discussion two important works, not properly 'concertos': the *Water Music* and the *Music for the Royal Fireworks*. Both, while composed in Handel's distinctive anglicised Italo-German style, belong to an essentially French tradition of outdoor music, typified in the symphonies of men like Lalande and Mouret which were written to enliven the royal suppers, water parties and the like at Versailles.

For all its pre-eminence in popularity among Handel's works, the *Water Music*'s history and origins remain uncertain. It would take a book longer than this to sort out the problems surrounding the early editions and the text generally; and even the date (or dates) of composition are obscure. There is a famous anecdote, related by Handel's earliest biographer John Mainwaring, about Handel's being restored to George I's favour (after his truancy from Hanover when George was Elector there) by a water party on the Thames when the royal barge was serenaded. But it is doubtful whether Handel was ever seriously out of favour; and if he was, another anecdote, about the violinist Geminiani's demanding to be accompanied by him before the King, is just as plausible.

Still, it remains possible that the *Water Music*, or some of it, was heard at a royal river party on 22 August 1715, when the King and his party sailed from Whitehall to Limehouse, and were regaled with music on the return journey; versions of a few of the movements existed by then. It was certainly heard on such an occasion two years later. The event was reported in the *Daily Courant* of 19 July 1717:

On Wednesday [July 17] Evening, at about 8, the King took Water at Whitehall in an open Barge, wherein were also the Dutchess of Bolton, the Dutchess of Newcastle, the Countess of Godolphin, Madam Kilmanseck, and the Earl of Orkney. And went up the River towards Chelsea. Many other Barges with Persons of Quality attended, and so great a Number of Boats, that the whole River in a manner was cover'd; a City Company's Barge was employ'd for the Musick, wherein were 50 Instruments of all sorts, who play'd all the Way from Lambeth (while the Barges drove with the Tide without Rowing, as far as Chelsea) the finest Symphonies, compos'd express for this Occasion, by Mr. Hendel; which his Majesty liked so well, that he caus'd it to be plaid over three times in going and returning. At Eleven his Majesty went a-shore at Chelsea, where a Supper was prepar'd, and then there was another very fine Consort of Musick, which lasted till 2; after which his Majesty came again into his Barge, and return'd the same Way, the Musick continuing to play till he landed.

This information is supplemented by a report of the event from the Prussian Resident in London, Frederic Bonet, who recorded that

... Next to the King's barge was that of the musicians, about 50 in number, who played on all kinds of instruments, to wit trumpets, horns, hautboys, bassoons, German [transverse] flutes, French flutes [recorders], violins and basses; but there were no singers. The music had been composed specially by the famous Handel...

Various conjectures have been made about which movements

may or may not have been performed on which occasions; but the evidence is tenuous, and the most that can be said with certainty is that the instruments listed by Bonet tally with Handel's complete score, which might be taken to imply that the entire work (or not much short of it) was given. The *Water Music* breaks down into three groups of movements: in F, with oboes, bassoon and horns as well as strings; in D, for the same with trumpets; and in G (major and minor), with flutes or recorders or oboes – the same musicians normally played all three – and bassoon. (Possibly the D and G suites are really all one; in some sources the movements are intermingled.) It has been suggested that the F major music was played on the upstream journey, the G major/minor at supper (its more delicate scoring implies indoor performance), and the D major downstream; but unless our ideas on tempo or the *Daily Courant* facts are wildly awry, that cannot have been the case.

Of the three groups, the F major is the longest, and probably the earliest – the existence of two of the D major movements in F (*HG* xlvii, 2–15), in what are clearly earlier versions, suggests that the first *Water Music* was planned as a homogeneous collection in F. It begins with a formal French overture, the fugal section characteristically loose and lacking in contrapuntal rigour. After an *adagio*, designed to allow the oboist an opportunity for expressive improvisation, there is a sequence of movements of steadily decreasing complexity of structure. First, an *allegro* with punched-out repeated notes on the horns, answered by the rest of the orchestra; then a gentle D minor air, an *andante*, with oboes and bassoon in dialogue with strings; next a passepied or rapid minuet, with the horns quietly echoing each strain, and a D minor middle section for the strings. The second air is the emotional heart of the suite – a graceful, flowing melody with quiet hints of pathos, repeated with high horns adding a subtle gloss. Over the water, the effect must have been magical. Then follow some dance movements: a *minuet* (with a minor-key trio, in which the top line and the central one, doubled by the bassoon, are equally melodic; compare Op. 3 no. 4*a*, Ex. 6, p. 18), a rapid *bourrée* and a sturdy *hornpipe*. These last are marked to be played first by strings, then by wind, and then by tutti, though how this relates to the repeats of the two sections is uncertain. Should it be $A_1 A_2 A_3$, $B_1 B_2 B_3$? or $A_1 B_1$, $A_2 B_2$, $A_3 B_3$? or perhaps $A_1 A_2$, $B_1 B_2$, $A_3 B_3$?

A movement in D minor, missing from certain sources, is

usually placed after the F major pieces – not quite satisfactorily, though a logical enough link with the D major group. Its style, with the reed trio set against the strings, is rather like that of the D minor *andante*. The D major music begins with rousing trumpets in dialogue with horns and the string-woodwind tutti – a fine, clean-limbed piece, Handel at his most vigorously ceremonious. This movement is one which also exists in an F major version; the other is the famous *hornpipe*, which follows from it without break. Next (if the traditional D major grouping is followed) come a pair of movements whose heavy pomp is redolent of Versailles, a slow minuet and a *lentement*, and finally a brief *bourrée*.

The G major pieces are of quite a different kind – more like the ballet music in Handel's operas of the mid-1730s than anything else in the *Water Music*. Possibly that resemblance induced the editor of the Halle Handel Edition score to suggest that it may have been composed for a royal water party in 1736: a theory which does not stand up to critical examination, as some of the G major music was in print before that date. All the movements in G are dances. First is a triple-time movement with no tempo mark, more like a sarabande than a minuet. A flute softens the first violin line. Second is a *rigaudon*, very like a *bourrée*, which gains in vitality from the characteristically unorthodox rhythm of its melody. It has a minor-key middle section. The music stays in the minor for the perky little minuet which follows; this movement has a deliciously humorous trio – the nearest Handel came to composing a Viennese waltz – with a high-pitched recorder doubling the violins in an oddly angular melodic line:

Ex. 20

(middle parts omitted)

Last, a pair of brief movements more like country dances than anything else. The first (in G minor) uses the high recorder; the second (in G major) has another of those interior melodies, with ear teased over which line it should focus on. (It looks and sounds as though the first was intended as a 'trio' for the second, but there is no textual evidence to support the idea.) There is nothing to be found elsewhere in Handel's music to suggest the remotest influence of, or interest in, folk music.

The other great occasional piece dates from the opposite end of Handel's life. In 1748 the Peace of Aix-la-Chapelle was signed, and in celebration a firework display was planned for Green Park in April 1749. The King agreed to have music with it, but only for 'warlike instruments'. Handel was duly commissioned, but it is clear from the ensuing correspondence between the government officers in charge of the event that he proved intractable. At the last moment, instead of merely 'warlike instruments' (wind and percussion), he demanded strings – no doubt the ensemble and intonation problems of a vast wind band worried him. 'Now Hendel proposes to lessen the nomber of trompets, &c and to have violeens. I don't at all doubt but when the King hears it he will be very much displeased . . . I am shure it behoves Hendel to have as many trumpets, and other martial instruments, as possible, tho he dont retrench the violins, which I think he shoud, tho I beleeve he will never be persuaded to do it', wrote the Master of the Ordnance to the Comptrollor of his Majesty's Fireworks. Next, Handel objected to the notion of a public rehearsal in Vauxhall Gardens. He seems to have been overruled: one took place on 21 April, with an audience estimated at 12,000, and the resulting traffic jam blocked London Bridge for three hours.

Was he overruled on the 'violeens'? Did he 'retrench'? Some commentators believe that he did; but if the number of wind instruments specified in his score is calculated (24 oboes, 12 bassoons, 1 double bassoon, 9 each of horns and trumpets, timpani), it falls considerably short of the 'band of 100 musicians' reported in two different sources as having taken part. There could have been at least 40 string players. The only surviving score does in fact indicate the addition of strings, though the work is performable without them. What is certain is that a wind-only performance runs clean counter to Handel's wishes; his own later performances included strings, as did the text whose publication he authorised.

The fireworks themselves, on 27 April, were a mixed success; part of the specially erected building caught fire, and there was some rain. But the music, it seems, was well received. It is a short work in the traditional French-overture-and-dances pattern; the evidence of an early edition suggests that more movements, extracted from existing works, may have supplemented it. As usual with Handel, the French overture has a strong Anglo-Italian accent. This opening movement is one of his grandest and most masterly creations, the kind of music that can be written only by a supreme composer – and at a time when there was a universal, unshakeable confidence in a particular way of life. It may not, however, have been conceived specially for the occasion: there exist two workings of the same material (*HG* xlvii, 72, 80), earlier and simpler – possibly the works which they begin were initial drafts of the *Fireworks Music* or, likelier, were concertos for use in oratorio performances. The final version puts these into the shade for breadth and grandeur, and its orchestration of course gives greater scope, with brass in antiphony with the rest, or horns answering trumpets, to be capped by a huge tutti. Handel's three different harmonisations of the opening phrase demonstrate how, not content with blazing brass to make his effect, he called on every resource to surprise the listener into a realisation of the nobility of the occasion.

Ex. 21

bar 7

bar 37

The faster movement which follows seems to have been composed specially: the use of material which fits with the limitations of natural horns and trumpets, and offers exceptional opportunities for triple antiphony, suggests as much. The ear expects each phrase to be answered, but can never be sure in what colour, or in what combination of colours, the answer will be. Here again it is salutary to compare this movement with Handel's earlier attempts. The first was a fairly ordinary 3/4 movement, mostly in eight-bar or four-bar phrases. The second was a 3/4 fugue, not an un-impressive piece, but inducing a sense of anti-climax with its thin-textured start – inevitable in a fugue, of course – and its predictable continuation; while the trumpety arpeggio material with which Handel tries to escape from the fugal strait-jacket is little short of banal. The final version avoids such traps, though it includes the same 'banal' ideas (now less so because of their bigger context and more imaginative bass) and much other matter from the fugue of the second version. The movement is interrupted briefly by a return to French-overture material; then there is a shortened *da capo*.

First of the dances is a short *bourrée*, simply for two upper parts and bass, which is followed by a *siciliana* entitled 'La paix', richly scored, with independent horn parts. The next movement, 'La réjouissance', is not exactly a dance but a cheerful scurrying *allegro*: it is directed to be played three times – by trumpets, woodwind and strings, by horns and woodwind, and by everyone together. Finally, a pair of brief minuets: the first a D minor piece in simple three-part writing (its main theme is derived from the original second movement of the first version of the work, the one described above as 'fairly ordinary'), the second in D major, and fully scored in the same pattern as 'La réjouissance'. The *Music for the Royal Fireworks* should not be rated excessively high; it is an occasional piece, and bears the marks of it. But it also bears the imprint of a man of his time, who saw virtue in the British way of life of which by his own choice he partook, and hymned its victory with the full might of his genius.

Index of Works Discussed